MRS. COLERIDGE

Minnow among Tritons

MRS. S. T. COLERIDGE'S LETTERS

TO THOMAS POOLE

1799–1834

Edited by STEPHEN POTTER for the
NONESUCH PRESS 16 Great James Street
Bloomsbury
1934

LIST OF ILLUSTRATIONS

iii

PREFATORY NOTE

THESE letters, written by Coleridge's wife to Thomas Poole, of Nether Stowey, are printed from one of the Thomas Poole MS volumes in the British Museum (Add. 35,344). The text has not been difficult to follow, except for the occasional blotting out of words by a seal, occasional torn corners, and Mrs Coleridge's habit of saving space by writing her long postscripts crossways on top of page one—a characteristic, but, in pre-penny-black days, not a trivial, economy. The letters are printed *literatim*, and without omissions, except for the occasional correction of an ambiguity in punctuation, and the cutting short, on ten occasions, of Mrs Coleridge's often repeated enquiries after old Stowey friends.

KEY TO REFERENCES IN THE INTRODUCTION

A. Mrs Sandford, *Thomas Poole and his Friends*.
B. *Letters of S. T. Coleridge*, ed. E. H. Coleridge.
C. *Unpublished Letters of Samuel Taylor Coleridge*, ed. E. L. Griggs.
D. *Early Life of Southey*, W. Haller.
E. *Life of S. T. Coleridge*, J. Dykes Campbell.
F. MS. Add. 35,343.
G. *Early Recollections*, J. Cottle.
H. *Complete Poetical Works of S. T. Coleridge*, ed. E. H. Coleridge.
I. *Biographia Epistolaris*, ed. Turnbull.
J. Richard Reynell, *Illustrated London News*, 1893.
K. De Quincey, *Works*.
L. *T. Wedgwood*, R. B. Litchfield.
M. *Coleridge and Asra*. T. M. Raysor, *Studies in Philology*, July, 1929.
N. Shelley, *Letters*, ed. R. Ingpen.

O. Sir Walter Scott, *Familiar Letters*.
P. *Letters of the Wordsworth Family*, ed. Knight.
Q. *Dorothy Wordsworth*, E. de Selincourt.
R. S. T. Coleridge, *Anima Poetae*.
S. S. T. Coleridge, *Table Talk*, ed. T. Ashe.
T. MS. 341. National Library of Scotland.
U. *Coleridge at Highgate*, L. E. Watson
V. Daniel Stuart, *Gentleman's Magazine*, July, 1838.
W. Charles Lamb, *Letters*. E. V. Lucas.

My sincere thanks are due to Mr E. J. O'Brien for pointing out to me the accessibility of these letters, and the strange fact that they have not hitherto been published: to Mr J. I. M. Stewart, for allowing me to draw on his knowledge of MSS. relating to Coleridge: and to the Manuscript Department of the British Museum. I am fortunate to have been able again to benefit from the generous interest of Mr G. H. B. Coleridge, who in granting his permission for this publication let me reproduce illustrations from original portraits in his possession, and made it possible for me to study his own large collection of Mrs Coleridge's letters.

The ~~Boddington~~ Circassian's Love-chaunt.

High o'er the rocks at night I rov'd 2.
To forget the form, I lov'd.
Image of Lewti! from my mind
Depart! for Lewti is not kind.'

Bright was the Moon: the Moon's bright beam
Speckled with many a moving Shade,
Danc'd upon Tamaha's stream;
But brightlier on the Rock it play'd,
The Rock, half-shelter'd from my view
By pendent boughs of tressy Yew!
True to Love, but false to Rest,
My fancy whisper'd in my breast—
So shines my Lewti's forehead fair
Gleaming thro' her sable hair.
Image of Lewti! from my mind
Depart! for Lewti is not kind.

MS. (Add. 35, 343, f. 2) of Coleridge's poem *Lewti: or the Circassian
Love-chaunt.* For "Cora" (? representing Sara) Coleridge has substituted
the more impersonal "Lewti." "Cora" itself was an alteration from a
still earlier "Mary" (cf. p. x.).

INTRODUCTION

ONE of the problems likely to be illustrated by these letters is suggested at once by their dates. The earliest were written in 1799, when Coleridge was touring Germany with the Wordsworths—Mrs Coleridge is complaining of the absence of her husband and lamenting the death of her son Berkeley. The rest date from 1807, the year after Coleridge's return from Malta, when Mrs Coleridge must have realised, probably for the first time, that Coleridge was unalterably determined to leave her permanently. The whole series is connected, directly and indirectly, with the separation.

The importance of this marriage failure in the study of Coleridge needs some explanation for those who only know him as a man made up of inexplicably disconnected components, fascinating by his poetry, alternately stupefying and animating by his prose, and at the same time exemplifying, by famous weaknesses, a failure in the art of life. Continue the study a little further, and it may be that suddenly a main drift will be felt, a current in which all these apparent oppositions are seen to be floating along together, in jostling but natural association: and once this discovery has been made, Coleridge's life begins to seem more important than the isolated perfections of his published work.

The opportunities for the study of this life are almost inexhaustible. Coleridge is alive along so many lines, the ramifications of his sensitiveness are so wide, his powers of consciousness are so extensive, his instinct to record so constant. With Coleridge, because they are deeply felt and freely expressed, we seem to be reading about such crises as the death of a son, or the borrowing of a book, such states as marriage unhappiness, or unwillingness to answer a letter, as if they were happening for the first time. Intimate details—the present collection comes within the bounds of such a depreciatory title—are significant because they really are intimate, they really do touch Coleridge's life closely.

Nor is Coleridge the only witness. The Lake circle are absorbing not because they were unique but because they were articulate. Even quite ordinary people may be subject to the fascinating illumination of De Quinceys or Dorothy Wordsworths. Mrs Coleridge comes within this field, and as these letters show, the lake air stirred her tongue also. The fearful ardours of her marriage, and the question of the blame—if that is the question—will be found set forth from a new point of view.

In Mrs Coleridge's phrase, this is the history of the thing.

From Coleridge's point of view, the chief blame fell on Southey. 1794 was the first great year of Coleridge's youth. Age of Reason emancipations, undergraduate rebellions against church and state, wild-oats of bottle parties, and lady parties, running away and enlisting—all these embryo activities, plus a repentance and a self-castigation, were telescoped into the years 1792 and 1793. In 1794, Coleridge settled down, not to steady-going existence, nor a death of permanent emancipation, but to life, new growth, and the concentration of real youth.

The first shape which Coleridge assumed in the process of his evolution was idealist. 1794 is the year of Pantisocracy. He conceived that inward health depended on the external conditions of life, and that virtue was impossible except in a community where worldly concerns, such as profit, and mundane religions and morality, were left outside. Bearing with him these ideas and under full sail of

his peerless enthusiasm, he bore down on Bristol, and on
Southey.

Southey was to be his friend. A friend—what Coleridge
called a proto-friend—was associated with each new step
in his life. Southey found himself turned from a conven-
tionally promising young man with a general intention to
emigrate, into a leader of the Pantisocrats and keenest
Susquehannah man. It was Coleridge who, assured by a
friend of its freedom from Byson and hostile Indians, the
tameness of its Mosquitoes, and its financial rewards for
literary characters, had decided on the banks of the Susquehannah as the site for their society. Southey, for the
first and last time in his career, was content to be a dis-
ciple. His part was to suggest difficulties: Coleridge's,
superbly to over-ride them.

One of these difficulties arose almost at once, out of a
fundamental tenet of the Book of Pantisocracy. The
colony, to succeed, must multiply:

Twelve gentlemen of good education and liberal principles A. i. 97
are to embark with twelve ladies in April next. Previous to
their leaving this country they are to have as much intercourse
as possible, in order to ascertain each other's dispositions, and
firmly to settle every regulation for the government of their
future conduct.

The Pantisocrats needed mates. Southey was engaged
to a Miss Edith Fricker, who seemed perfectly to fit such a
description. Lovell, another member, was already married
to another of these Bristol Miss Frickers. Coleridge
was unattached. With the general and undetailed glance
of idealism, Coleridge chose Sara, one of the three remaining sisters, for himself: without the convention of
an engagement, it was known, in August of this year 1794,
that Sara was to be his—a sisterhood for the fraternity.

Coleridge departed for London. He was too absorbed
in his Cause to be an ardent correspondent, but when he

returned to Cambridge for his last term he wrote in enthusiastic, if general, terms (not to Sara, but to Southey):

B. 81 America! Southey! Miss Fricker! Yes, Southey, you are right. Even Love is the creature of strong motive. I certainly love her. I *think* of her incessantly and with unspeakable tenderness,— with that inward melting away of soul that symptomatizes it.

Coleridge had known his future wife for rather more than two months.

Yet within a day of writing the letter, the precarious certainty was infected with doubt. Coleridge, in these years of his life, is strong in action. But even in this period of his youth, if the motive for action were suggested by somebody else, if it took any shape remotely resembling that of Duty, his powers faded. Crossing his own, a letter from Southey arrived suggesting that his friend should be more assiduous in his letters to Bristol and not so general, when he did write, in sending his regards to the Frickers.

Coleridge was stung, not of course into renewed love for Sara, but into philosophic reflections on the subject
B. 82 of rectitude. "There may be too high a state of health, perhaps even *virtue* is liable to a *plethora* . . . Your undeviating simplicity of rectitude has made you rapid in decision . . . There is *phlogiston* in your heart . . ." He had already written to Sara, but she seems suddenly to have assumed an ominous quality, from which he cannot escape. Coleridge at this time is a necessitarian: Miss Fricker seems to have taken on the lineaments of a Fate.

At once, Coleridge looks round as if for escape. He is fascinated, perhaps because he has not the right to be
B. 95 fascinated, by a Miss Brunton. And then, at the precise moment of maximum effectiveness, comes a letter from Mary Evans. If he did not realise it fully before, he realises it fully now—that he has always loved Mary Evans, whom he has known for years, but for whom he may per-

haps have felt at first only a feeling of romantic affection, connecting her with the happiness of his youth—"oh from sixteen to nineteen what hours of paradise had Allen and I in escorting the Miss Evanses home on a Saturday, who were then at a milliners"— E. 15

Mary Evans writes to him on the subject of Pantisocracy. She speaks deprecatingly, with an ambiguous personal appeal, and restrained warmth. The letter transforms Coleridge from spontaneous advocate of an ideal into a man grimly hanging on, into a martyr. She has written about the "Plan so absurd and extravagant": B. 87

For whom am I now violating the rules of female delicacy? Is it for the same Coleridge, whom I once regarded as a sister her best-beloved Brother? . . . There is an Eagerness in your Nature, which is ever hurrying you in the sad Extreme . . . You have doting Friends! Will you break their hearts? . . .

Coleridge copies this out and sends it in a letter to Southey. "I loved her, Southey, almost to madness." The need for reclaiming Coleridge is more urgent than ever.

For Coleridge, of course, the engagement to Miss Fricker became more uncompromisingly than ever a thing of duty. Yet so great is the power of youth, a condition which Coleridge fully possessed, that such a dispiriting situation even as this could be translated into something positive, not to say enjoyable. He relished the situation of frustrated love, and marriage from duty. He was in the midst of discovering Schiller, and the German romantics. His face is sternly set, he says. He writes a Sonnet—"Thou bleedest, my poor Heart!" a poem eventually printed with the title *On a Discovery Made too Late*. He encloses it in a letter to a friend—"It was occasioned by a letter, which I C. i. 28 lately received from a young Lady, whom for five years I loved—almost to madness,—dissuasive from my American Scheme—but where Justice leads, I will follow— though the Path be through thorns and roughness—The

Scotts desire their Compliments. *Compliments!* Cold aristo-
cratic Inanities! I abjure their Nothingness." Though the
sorrow is sincere, such strength of youthful spirits and
pleasure in experience seems more to be envied than pitied.

But this grandeur of unhappiness was closely dependent
on the grandeur of Coleridge's great ideal. A less splendid,
and therefore less bearable kind of disappointment was in
store for him. The first burst of Pantisocracy was beginning
to expend itself. Enthusiasm was no longer so fresh—and
what made things worse was that the defection, it seemed
to Coleridge, was coming from Southey. It was not that
Southey was losing interest—on the contrary his letters to
Coleridge on the subject are assiduous. It was the kind of
detail he stuck out for which Coleridge did not like. His
failure to keep the plan in its original state of all-or-
nothing. Southey had already raised the question, for instance—should Shadrach Weekes accompany them (he was
the servant of Southey's aunt). Coleridge had superbly
B. 82 overridden this difficulty. "SHAD GOES WITH US. HE IS MY
BROTHER." But now Southey wrote that the servants would
be expected to perform that part of labour for which their
B. 90 education had fitted them. "*Southey* should not have
written that sentence," Coleridge answered. Rectitude is
no bad defence against rectitude, and Southey was still
calling his friend to duty. Coleridge had not at first been
averse to Southey's idea that a mother and a mother-in-
law should be in the Susquehannah party. "If Mrs Southey
and Mrs Fricker go with us," Coleridge agrees, "they can
at least prepare the food of simplicity for us." But later on
B. 98 he began to doubt Southey's wisdom here also. "I wish,
Southey, in the stern severity of judgment, that the two
mothers were *not* to go, and that the children stayed with
them . . . *That* Mrs Fricker! We shall have her teaching
the infants *Christianity*."

At the end of the year (December 1794) Coleridge lapses,
temporarily but completely. The rumour that Mary Evaps

is betrothed shocks him into some realisation of the situation, and fills him with despair. He writes to know his fate —a letter which if it had been answered as he seemed to hope, would presumably have ended Pantisocracy and certainly all Bristol connections. But the rumour is true, and Coleridge has to set his face finally for duty and Sara Fricker. At first he cannot face it. He disappears to London. No-one at Bristol hears from him. He is said to be with Lamb at the *Salutation and Cat*. Letters from Southey find him. He promises to arrive at Bristol on a certain day, and breaks his promise. He appoints a meet- D. 150 ing place some weeks later—Southey and Lovell walk twenty miles to meet an empty coach.

At last, urged no doubt by insistent voices in the rear, Southey goes up to London to find Coleridge at the *Angel* Inn, draws him off to Bristol, the reconciliation sets in, very soon Coleridge has "re-commenced ardent lover and Pantisocrat". The betrothal becomes formal. Friendship with Southey is resumed. Perhaps warm-hearted sympathy for Sara has influenced him; perhaps she charms him: perhaps he has been able to recapture the excitement of the sensation that he is acting for the sake of a Cause. A letter illuminates Coleridge's character at this time, and to some extent Sara's also:

I consider myself as under particular ties of gratitude to her C. i. 30 —since in confidence of Affection she has rejected the Addresses of two Men, one of them of large Fortune. . . . she vainly endeavours to conceal from me how heavy her heart is with anxiety . . . In short, why should I write circuitously to you? So commanding are the requests of her Relations, that a short Time must decide whether she marries me whom she loves with an affection to the ardor of which my Deserts bear no proportion—or a man whom she strongly dislikes, in spite of his fortune and solicitous attentions to her. These peculiar circumstances she had with her usual delicacy concealed from me till my arrival at Bristol . . .

Introduction

Coleridge married Sara Fricker on October 4th, 1795. In the summer of that year he was addressing her affectionately in his poetry—"My pensive Sara! . . . My Sara—best beloved of human kind!" There seems to have been love—even deep attachment between them for a time. Coleridge had managed to act for perhaps the first and certainly for the last time in his life as he "ought", in the world's eye, to have acted.

But he was never able to forgive the world's instrument, Southey. By autumn the impulse of Pantisocracy had evaporated. The direction of Coleridge's development had completely altered. The libel went that Southey had no desire to share out a newly acquired and much needed legacy—and Coleridge wrote a long and angry letter to his friend, as if all the blame were his: as if Southey had failed him. Of Sara he says that he loves, is beloved, and is happy: but nevertheless the real grievance was not the defection from Pantisocracy, but the visit to London at the beginning of the year, the summoning to duty. "And was not this your own plan," he writes with a bitterness

B. 147 which lived through all subsequent reconciliations, "was not this your plan—the plan for the realising of which you invited me to Bristol: the plan for which I abandoned my friends, and every prospect, and every certainty, and the woman whom I loved to an excess which you in your warmest dream of fancy could never shadow out?" And years later, when he neither loved nor was beloved, when

H. 1050 the affectionate verses to Sara had been edited, and "Cora" was changed to "Lewti" in the poem, he returned to the thought of this bitterness, and the realisation once again

C. i. 404 that he "cut the throat of his own happiness, of his genius, of his utility, in compliment to the merest phantom of overstrained honour—O Southey, Southey, what an unthinking man were you, and unjust!"

In spite of the fearful auguries of its inception, the mar-

xiv

riage turned out, at first, to be a happy one. Coleridge's G. J.
supplies of youth were so vast that the novelty of the situation, even if he had felt no love, would have been enough
to make him happy. Three days after the marriage Coleridge confides in a new friend, Thomas Poole of Nether
Stowey: "On Sunday morning I was *married* . . . We are F. 83
settled—nay—quite domesticated at Clevedon—our comfortable cot!!—Mrs Coleridge—MRS COLERIDGE!! I
like to *write* the name:" Coleridge is enjoying the difficulties of poverty and inexperience. He writes to Cottle and
asks for "a riddle slice; a candle box; two ventilators; two G.
glasses for the wash-hand stand; one tin dust pan; . . . a
bible; a keg of porter". Quite soon the charm of the actual
poverty began to pall; Marriage, he says, has taught him C. i. 48
the wonderful uses of the vulgar article of life *Bread*.
Particularly as he had to make a small contribution to Mrs
Fricker's household, when, as he admits, he was conscious
of "five mouths opening and shutting as I pull the string".
He is occasionally hampered, still, by the sense of duty.
His wife with child, and he forced to write to support her
. . . "write the flights of poetic enthusiasm, when every
minute I am hearing a groan from my wife"—the scene
for Coleridge sometimes lacks grandeur, even though he
can say "The future is cloud and thick darkness", and
"Poverty . . . the thin faces of them that want bread, look- B. 155
ing up at me". Nevertheless, these are the words of a
happy man. And soon a new excitement of experience is
to absorb him. He becomes a father. Hartley is born
(September, 1796)—dignity and interest is restored. He
makes Hartley an object of his new development, his new
powers of apprehension, and records observations of the
child in notes and letters: at the same time, true to his
character, he expands and declaims in the new situation,
and tells Poole how he looks upon the infant "with a B. 169
melancholy gaze",—all youth and happiness still.

Following on this, there were the new relationships and

the new experiences attendant on the move to Nether
Stowey. Close association with a wonderful new friend,
Poole—and then with the Wordsworths. A great accession
of life in Coleridge, rendering him newly articulate, and
capable of poetry almost as if for the first time. The kind
of site for his cottage he had always wanted. It must even
have seemed that Pantisocracy, on the more limited lines
of the family as a unit, had been achieved at last, with
Coleridge determined to turn to what he called "hus-
bandry" and support everybody by digging up his garden.
With all these things Mrs Coleridge is still associated:
I. i. 123 "We are all—wife, bratling, and self, remarkably well.
Mrs Coleridge likes Stowey, and loves Thomas Poole and
his mother, who love her. A communication has been
B. 216 made from our orchard into T. Poole's garden . . ." "*We
are no common people*," he says in a letter to a friend, a
month later. And then, after that (February, 1797), the
friendly or affectionate references to his wife (when he is
writing to a third person) begin to stop. The door into
Poole's garden was to become a kind of symbol of the
gradual, the very prolonged withdrawal of Coleridge from
what he slowly began to regard as the encumbrance of his
family.

His devotion to his own house had never been exclusive,
even in the earliest days of his marriage; within a few
weeks of it they had moved out of the isolation of Clevedon cottage to be nearer the Redcliffe library and Bristol
Society: within six months Coleridge was away in the
Midlands on his long tour with the prospectus of the
A. *Watchman*. Then, at the end of 1796, there comes the extraordinary series of letters to Poole, when Coleridge was
negotiating for the house at Nether Stowey. It seems to
him that Poole, then beginning to take position as first-
friend, is not sufficiently enthusiastic at the prospect of
the Coleridges as neighbours. Poole has written to say
that the only cottage available is not big enough. He

doubts Coleridge's powers with the garden; he suggests Acton. Coleridge feels the ground cut from under his feet. "The tumult of my spirits has now subsided, but the B. 187 Damp struck into my very heart; and there I feel it. O my God! my God! where am I to find rest? Since I have returned I have been poring into a book, as a show for not looking at my wife and the baby. By God, I dare not look at them. Acton! The very name makes me grind my teeth." Coleridge had discovered in Thomas Poole, as others were to discover, an unusual mixture. He was a respected and popular country gentleman, adept in the business and pleasures of an estate, and at the same time a hero-worshipper—as well as a connoisseur—of genius. More important for Coleridge, his chief interest was in the kind of discussions—on the nature of life and the real problems of philosophy—which at this time and for the rest of his life were to absorb Coleridge himself. The strange exaggeration of Coleridge's language is almost certainly due to his half-conscious sense of the imperious necessity, for him, of this kind of companionship.

It was the kind he could not get from his wife. Mrs Coleridge was not a stupid woman, but it was beginning to seem to her husband as if her problems were exclusively worldly ones, his exclusively not. It would certainly be difficult to attempt to reconstruct conversations between Coleridge and his friends—on the doctrine of necessity, Spinoza, or the meaning of miracles—in which she could take part. Of how she did come in, on occasion, there is one slight clue to suggest. Coleridge is in the middle of a quarrel with Southey. Coleridge accuses Southey of being hypocritical when he says, in the midst of "heart-chilling sentiments", that his affection for Coleridge is unaltered. When you uttered those words, Coleridge reminds him, do you not remember how your answer B. 150 startled Sara, so that she "affronted you into angry silence by exclaiming 'What a story!'" Sara's remark seems inadequate to such Homeric warfare: later on she must have felt herself a minnow among the Tritons of the Lakes, and *Cf.* 139 her silence, in such company, would have grown.

Mrs Coleridge was fond of Poole, and probably did not object to whatever desertions he was the cause of. The counter-attraction of the Wordsworths was something quite different. Coleridge's discovery of the Wordsworths was the great event of this decade. They were the friends associated with his period of fullest life. The three friends, in their discussions, were exchanging worlds. Self-evolution and self-discovery could have nothing to do with a woman struggling with the difficulties of housekeeping, and Mrs Coleridge was conscious that, intellectually, she had to see herself measured against Dorothy. De Quincey, with a somewhat journalistic eye for family detail, has emphasised the likelihood of this qualified jealousy, and tells a story of how Dorothy, for a joke, once annoyed Mrs Coleridge, when they all came in out of the rain, by K. ii. 64 dressing up in her clothes, "making herself merry with her own uncerimoniousness and Mrs Coleridge's gravity". Coleridge went off on a visit to the Wordsworths at Racedown, without her. When the Wordsworths settled at Alfoxden—their motive, the enjoyment of Coleridge's society—mutual visits took place almost daily. There was the walking tour to the Valley of Rocks, the preparation and publication of the *Lyrical Ballads*. Then finally, and, as it turned out, irretrievably, there was the tour in Germany. It was originally intended that Mrs Coleridge should come too. Next, that she should join them some time later.

She remained behind, alone. Four months before he left, Coleridge's second son, Berkeley, was born. Coleridge tried to make amends for his absence by ending up his B. 277 long, if infrequent messages with "Oh my dear Babies! my Babies!" But the main body of his letter was always full of pleasures and social delights. The baby was ill, and

xviii

Mrs Coleridge was badly in need of the presence of a husband, at the same time dreading the explosion of exaggerated feelings which she knew any bad tidings would call forth.

In February, Berkeley died. To spare Coleridge, neither Poole nor Sara wrote to tell him of this till March. All that his wife asked was that he should keep to his promise of returning in May. Coleridge wrote a long, feeling letter. He tried to mend his conscience by writing some rather inadequate verses:

> Death whisper'd. With assenting Nod H. 312
> Its head upon the Mother's breast
> The baby bow'd, and went without demur . . .

But the fatal "*ought to*" kept him away. He did not return to Stowey till July.

The death of Berkeley was the end of an era for Mrs Coleridge. She could never forget him, or her grief. "To B. 282 behold the death of a child—", she wrote to Coleridge, "it is a suffering beyond your conception . . . I have seen him twice at the brink of the grave, but he has returned and recovered and smiled upon me like an angel." On the back of this letter she wrote many years afterwards: "No secrets herein. I will not burn it for the sake of my sweet Berkeley". She mentions him, most often, in these letters to Poole. His death seems to have meant for her the end of pleasant days at Stowey, the end of kind Mr Poole and his garden, the end of happy married life. Coleridge, conscious of most things, seems to realise this too when he says:

There are moments in which I have such a power of life B. 296 within me, such a *conceit* of it, I mean, that I lay the blame of my child's death to my absence. *Not intellectually*; but I have a strange sort of sensation, as if, while I was present, none could die whom I entirely loved.

Coleridge has chosen a new way of life, in which his

family are not included. In the background of this new kind of activity stand the Wordsworths. The earliest letters in this volume speak of the death of Berkeley. Mrs Coleridge's tone, when she mentions the *Lyrical Ballads* in the postscripts, is comprehending and comprehensible.

There is not much record of the state of affairs between the two in the first year after the return from Germany; but as soon as the Coleridges moved to Keswick, mutual dissatisfactions were apparent. The first confidential confession to a third person that his marriage is unhappy was sent—with dramatic justice—to Southey. He starts the

C. i. 182 letter: "Oct. 21. 1801—The day after my birthday—29 years of age! *Who on earth can say that without a sigh!*" and then goes on with complaints about his health, within which the actual reference is, with characteristic unpremeditation, contained.

The least agitation brings on bowel complaints, and within the last week *twice* with an ugly symptom—namely of sickness even to vomiting—and Sara—alas! we are not suited to each other . . .

Not, of course, with any hint of separation—but the converse of it is there, an affirmation that he is deeply convinced of the indissolubility of marriage. (In the Book of Pantisocracy the only question was to be whether a divorce could be made valid by the wish of one, or the agreement of both parties.) A little later, he is writing to Southey again:

B. 366 For what is life, gangrened, as it is with me, in its very vitals, domestic tranquillity?

In 1802 his feelings are definite enough, and loveless
L. 126 enough for him to say to a comparative stranger—"And there I had the misfortune to meet with my wife". The crisis seems to develop quickly. Coleridge confides in his friends. Some readjustment is essential.

Introduction

What steps does Coleridge take? Readers who are unfamiliar with his character, and the apparent contradictions of godlike super-humanity intermittently eclipsed by the all-too-human; readers who are unsympathetic to the sacred phenomena of such paradoxes, must read with Olympian or incredulous laughter.

He explains to Mrs Coleridge the limitations of her character. He explains how, whereas he himself has no Pride, dislikes gentility, is connected with the outside world by the pleasurable sense of its immediate Beauty, she, on the other hand, is controlled by the criterion of the average value of things in the minds of people in general. "The Eye and the Ear are your great organs, and you de- C. i. 190 pend upon the eyes and ears of others for a great part of your pleasures. . . ."

Or he enumerates her faults, supplementing advice on how they may be overcome:

2. Permit me, my dear Sara, without offence to you, as C. i. 221 Heaven knows! it is without any feeling of pride in myself, to say, that in six acquirements, and in the quantity and quality of natural endowments whether of feeling, or of intellect, you are the inferior . . . If you read this letter with half the tenderness with which it is written, it will do you and both of us *good* . . .

He checks himself. Perhaps the weak woman will need the help of some small psychological device to help her:

You know Sally Pally! I must have a joke or it would not be me!

It is all completely loveless, though there are efforts to be otherwise. When his wife is about to give birth, he starts off with solicitude—"I write with trembling—at C. i. 227 what time or in what state my letter may find you, how can I tell? . . . I trust in God . . ." and then—the real business of the letter. See that the best bedroom is aired for

T. Wedgwood, when he comes, and that his favourite kind of butter is in the house.

At other times, he speaks of a separation, and then is B. 389 pleased at the improved behaviour of his wife—she is made serious at last, he comments, under the shadow of this threat. Later, in 1803, he becomes more specific in his C. i. 238 advice, and warns her against jealousy—"suffer me to love and to be beloved without pain". Example—her coldness to the Wordsworths.

Or he takes refuge in tremendous complaints to sym-C. i. 215 pathisers and fellow-thinkers like Tom Wedgwood: "If any woman wanted an exact and copious Recipe," how to make a husband completely miserable, "I could her furnish with one—with a *Probatum est*, tacked on to it. Ill-tempered Speeches sent after me when I went out of the House, ill-tempered Speeches on my return, my friends received with freezing looks." But he has no plan. "O dear Sir! no one can tell what I have suffered. I can say with strict truth, that the happiest half-hours I have had, were when all of a sudden, as I have been sitting alone in my Study, I have burst into tears . . ." And then, as a further bewilderment, whenever he is away from her, feelings of what he owes to a wife, emotions of reminiscence, of pity, even of affection, begin to distress him, and he writes to C. i. 299 her with an overflowing remorse—my dear Sara! believe me . . . I am always planning for you . . . "nor is it possible that any name can be more awfully affecting, or sink into my heart . . . with a greater weight of duty . . ." Clevedon —Bristol—Nether Stowey, cannot be forgotten. And B. 468 again—"what we have been to each other, our understand-standing will not permit our hearts to forget". It seemed almost as if they might find common ground again in their C. i. 275 mutual unhappiness: "O Sara! dear Sara! try for all good things in the spirit of unsuspecting Love, for miseries gather upon us".

In the end, Coleridge compromised. He decided to

spend a year in the south—Madeira, perhaps. For two
years he had been making up his mind, and talking of the
"benefit to his health" which he hoped would be brought
about by removal from the damp mountain and the
damper domestic air of the lakes. A "vacation from house- C. i. 194
hold Infelicity", he once called it. In the autumn of 1804
he set sail at last, for Malta.

When he returned, in 1806, it might have been expected
that now, at any rate, he should have been able to decide
on a clear course of action. But the situation had been
made more complex and yet more cutting, more indeterminate and yet more crucial by the development of two
elements—Coleridge's love for Sara Hutchinson, and the
persistent difficulties made by his wife.

In 1799, Coleridge had fallen in love. He confessed it,
as he confessed everything, to his notebooks. "*Tunc tem-* M.
poris," he wrote, "*tunc primum amor me levi spiculo,*
venenato eheu et insanabili . . ." supply the dangerous
word—then love wounded me—"*me, manum a tergo*
longum in tempus prensatam..." *Prensatam* or *prensantem,*
the poisoner of the dart, and the owner of the hand he
held he names "Sara".

It is not Sara Fricker ("Christ! what a name for Cole- C. ii. 122
ridge to be transferred to!") but Sara Hutchinson, the
sister of the wife of his best friend, who was soon to become an almost permanent member of the Wordsworth
household. For six years—before he ever left England for
the Mediterranean—this love had been an antidote to the
unromantic round of quarrels and petty thwartings which
had been his life at Keswick. There is nothing here of the
pleasant melancholies or the moody brow of the Mary
Evans affair. Although it was to him something unattain-
able, though he had a fatal sense of the impossibility for
him of this kind of happiness, he was not merely in love
with the romance of love, much less was it an instance of
Coleridge finding "ought not" as provocative of action as

"ought" was preclusive. His love was most real, and like all his experience it received the richest statement, in poems like *Love*, still more in notebook sentences—thoughts unfortunately never included in *Anima Poetae*. His plans beyond accomplishment and preparations for an unrealisably great work—all have reference to this Sara: "Every thing that has been known or has been deemed fit to win woman's love, I have an impulse to make myself, even tho' I should otherwise look down upon it. I cannot endure not to be strong in arms, a daring soldier—yet I know I have no fear of life, or dread of pain, and that I am not that because I cannot respect it. Again I must be the high intellect that despises it, and both at once." At Malta her image becomes more distinct than ever, and his thoughts, when they relax, settle always back to her— "and while I am talking of government or war, or chemistry, there comes ever into my bodily eye some tree beneath which we have rested, some rock where we have stood on the projecting road edging high above the Crumnock Lake, when we sate beneath the Rock, and those dear lips pressed my forehead—or that Scale Force in its pride as we saw it when they laughed at us for two lovers." It was certain that when Coleridge returned from Malta, the chances of reconciliation with his wife would be more remote than ever.

After many delays, and much gathering together of his nervous resources, Coleridge paid a visit to Keswick. The return to old irritations quickly sickened him, and he determined to make a final, unqualified break. The Wordsworths encouraged him in this step: and in an attempt to make it irrevocable, he not only broached his wife, but stated the whole case to his brother, the Rev. George Coleridge, a man of advice and finality. In spite of her good qualities, Coleridge writes, Sara's "temper and general tone of feeling . . . I have found wholly incompatible with even an endurable life, and such as to preclude all

M.

C. i. 369

xxiv

chance of my ever developing the talents which my Maker has entrusted to me . . ." But the situation dragged on still further, remaining ruinously indeterminate, partly from the distraction of his love, partly from the opposition of Mrs Coleridge.

The motives of this opposition are difficult at first to consider seriously, though the free and unselfconscious revelation of character which these letters to Poole reveal may provoke the necessary sympathy. They at any rate present a credible point of view. According to Shelley, it is true, "Mrs Southey was stupid, and her sister, Mrs Cole- N. i. 209 ridge was worse". Shelley does not mean this: he despises their domesticity. Mrs Coleridge has several supporters— U. 92 Cottle, Mrs Gillman, and Poole. Walter Scott called her O. ii. 342 "a pleasing person, and has been pretty". (Prettiness of K. ii. 60 rather a commonplace order, De Quincey added.) Dorothy Wordsworth is the best authority, but she is naturally unsympathetic. When she calls Sara a "sad fiddle-faddler", Q. 128 on the strength of the length of time she takes to get the children dressed in the morning, we must regard it, after reading Sara's account of a typical Greta Hall day (in letter 16), as prejudice. But when Dorothy calls her the "lightest, weakest, silliest woman", because she is not Q. 131 serious enough to answer a serious letter, we recognise a particle of truth, from Dorothy's point of view: and after reading the letters here we can agree that she is "full of trouble" but that "one trouble wipes away another"—and understand Dorothy's quick corollary—"One comfort, P. ii. 12 that nothing hurts her".

Therefore Dorothy speaks with authority when she gives her opinion of Mrs Coleridge's reason for wishing to avoid the separation. Against it, she says, Mrs Coleridge "urges the one argument that this person, and that Q. 210 person, and everybody will talk". Coleridge repeats this when he tells his brother George that his wife's unwillingness is due to the fact that it will "not look *respectable* for her": and it is true that the appearances of the word "respectable" in these letters are only exceeded numerically by the word "prudent".

D. 44 In defence of Mrs Coleridge it must be pointed out that the Fricker sisters had certain ideals—that they were probably sent into the world with certain unforgettable warnings. Mr Fricker had died bankrupt in 1786, leaving his widow and six children penniless. The extreme importance of money must have been well emphasised on her daughters by the mother (the one whom Southey wished to include among the Pantisocrats). She herself at one time kept a school, and her daughters were educated well beyond the minimum scale of intelligence necessary to matrimony. Mary (afterwards Mrs Lovell) was an actress, and at the age of 90 is said to have kept up her Latin by reading Horace and her French by reading Mme de Staël. The two unmarried sisters, Eliza and Martha, earned their own living competently up to the end of their life. The two pretty ones, Edith and Sara, were more obviously meant for successful marriage. Edith did perfectly with the brilliant Southey, and loved her husband devotedly—even idolatrously—all through her life: Sara seemed equally well placed with the more brilliant though always less moneyed Coleridge. Southey steadily progressed—Edith was happy.

As year succeeded year Sara, on the other hand, had to admit that she had been less lucky. Unlike Southey, Coleridge was the last person in the world to give any woman the comfortable sense that she possessed a reliable background of husband; and his success as an earner was fearfully delayed—the economic conditions which Sara had been brought up to consider so important were not even tolerable: and all this was the more irritating to a wife who was constantly being congratulated on her marriage K. ii. 62 to a genius. As de Quincey says: "Hearing from everybody that Coleridge was a man of most extraordinary endowments . . . she naturally looked to see, at least, an ordinary measure of worldly consequence attend upon their exercise". No wonder she regarded Southey with such regretful admiration—Southey, who had lived at Greta Hall since 1803, and was the real head of her household—Southey, now steaming majestically ahead for the laureateship. No wonder she writes of him as she does in letter 13, perhaps the only critic who has preferred *The Lay of the Laureate* to *Kubla Khan*. No wonder, also, that 47 in 1806 all this adds to the irritation of Coleridge himself, who writes of her "self-encouraged admiration for P. 267 Southey, as a vindictive feeling in which she delights herself as satirizing me . . ."

And now, finally, Mrs Coleridge finds that her husband seriously intends to desert her. On top of other troubles, she is about to lose the small worldly consequence of her position as a married woman. Her opposition is understandable, but from its very motive, the truly moral necessity for Coleridge is made plain—that he must at all costs break away. Now or never he must act firmly.

"Now" however, happens to be 1807, a time when Coleridge is less able to act with simplicity or directness than at any other time in his life. He is beginning his last and most perilously uncontrolled period of drug addiction, when his inherent traits of procrastination, and allied faults, begin to be exaggerated almost to maniac proportions; he is about to become, for the time being, a "case", when capable friends should have come forward, as they had done in similar circumstances in the past and were to do again frequently in the future, and firmly take on the control of his affairs for him.

There was the reverend George—but in answer to his brother's letter he had shown a tendency to lecture, and his anxious discussions behind the back of the patient with other Coleridge brothers became food for Coleridge's incipient persecution mania. There was only one man who could help him—Wordsworth; but the situation in the Wordsworth family was complicated by Sara Hutchinson, for whom Coleridge's love had grown deeper and more despairing than ever since his return from Malta. It was further increased by proximity; for Coleridge, unable to face Keswick, was generously offered Rydal Mount as a home. It was offered sympathetically, and for the sake of

P. Q. the past. To the Wordsworths, the Coleridge who returned from Malta was not the old Coleridge. His eloquence trembles, now, on the brink of loquacity: he talks more to avoid reality than to make reality more conscious: and his intense interest in everything seemed to have disappeared. And he was altered in person. He was much aged, he had an unhealthy fatness—"like a dropsy". Coleridge must have suspected pity almost before it appeared, and yet all the time he is absorbed in despairing love: Love fills him, he says—so that every fibre of his heart

M. "seems to tremble under its perpetual touch and sweet pressure, like the string of a lute—with a sense of vibrating pain . . . that seems to shiver and tremble on the threshold of some joy that cannot be entered into while I am embodied—a pain of yearning which all the pleasure on earth could not induce me to relinquish, even were it in my power; and yet it *is* a pain, an aching, that spreads even into the eyes, that have a look as if they were asking a what and a where even of vacancy . . ." To help Coleridge now, the Wordsworths would have had to accept his love for Sara.

M. Their reserves of patience and loyalty were not equal to this. "It is not the Wordsworths' knowledge of my frailties that prevents my *entire* love of them. No! it is their ignorance of the deep place in my being—and O the cruel, cruel, misconception of that which is purest in me, which alone is indeed pure—my love of ασρα." Coleridge found himself being forced into solitude, a condition of which he was not capable. Even Sara must have begun to defect.

Under the fatal handicap of failure, appearing in that least attractive of all characters, the inactive-introspective, he found himself set beside the controlled effectiveness of Wordsworth, until at last admiration turned to jealousy. He would observe some small gesture—Sara Hutchinson taking Wordsworth's arm, perhaps, or siding with him in an argument, and he would write it down—for at this time his notebooks were his only confidants—"O agony! M. O the vision of that Saturday morning . . . O cruel! is he not beloved, adored by two—and two such beings, and must I not be beloved *near* him except as a satellite. But O mercy! mercy! is he not better, greater, more *manly*, and altogether more attractive to any the purest woman . . . awakened from a dream of tears, and anguish of involuntary jealousy, ½ past 2. Sept. 13. 1807." Help from the Wordsworths was impossible.

The famous quarrel, then, was not a business of chance. Indeed it was foreshadowed two years earlier, in 1808. Q. But when the impatient word—that Coleridge had for years been a positive "nuisance" in the Wordsworth household—was repeated to him it is difficult to conceive how he was able to support it. The casting himself loose from the Wordsworths in 1810 was the most agonising, the most uncompromising action of Coleridge's life. There was a reconciliation, but, as Mrs Coleridge says, there was never again to be *that* between them: and the 16 fact that he included Sara Hutchinson in the ban with such apparent irrationality simply shews that he knew, instinctively, that Wordsworth was preferred to him as an object of loyalty.

The completeness of the break was in the end a good thing for Coleridge. He visited Keswick again after it—dramatically ignoring the Wordsworths as he passed near their house. But the casting off from the Wordsworths meant the final casting off from Mrs Coleridge. It was only the happy secret of his love for the other Sara that had

made the later degradation of the marriage routine possible at all. Coleridge never visited the Lakes after 1812.
And from that date he made a recovery—of self-control,
self-respect, and powers of self-expression almost unbe-
lievable considering the depths to which he had sunk.

For the rest—Mrs Coleridge's complaints begin to stop.
The references to S. T. C. become fewer and fewer. She
turns to motherhood, and is absorbed in the careers of her
children, in the reform of her daughter Sara's health, and
of her son Hartley's morals, finding comfort, among these
many crises, in the comparative mediocrity of Derwent.
Many years later, she begins to speak of her husband
again, with a faintly bewildered curiosity. She has heard
some of the very young men speak of him with an extraordinary admiration—her son-in-law, H. N. Coleridge, for
instance—almost as if he were a great writer. She mentions to Poole, as something worth mentioning, that a
certain acquaintance "liked the *Ancient Mariner*".

Coleridge, for his part, found new friends—the
Morgans, and then the Gillmans, to help him through a
period of convalescence which involved the healing of
every possible kind of wound. It was a question of patch-
ing up rather than of regeneration. Coleridge was never
able to escape the particular trait, or group of traits, in
his character which made him make the initial mistake of
marrying Sara Fricker in order to conform to what the
least important part of the world thought was right. He
R. was what he called "that miserablest of widowers, an unhappy husband," all through his life. The world would
not let him forget it. A man who seems to set himself up
as a teacher of youth, with aids to reflection and states-
men's manuals, must not give to the antagonistic critics
so obvious a handle for abuse as "infidelity"—a handle
used with all the more glee because Coleridge was quite
incapable of taking such attacks with any kind of philosophic dignity. Fantastic libels were composed: *e.g.*,

Lockhart told the story that he had once been told the story—(and by Wordsworth)—that Coleridge "was ex- T. pelled from Greta Hall for getting Southey's maids with child one after another"—as if the truly passionate Coleridge could ever have behaved so breezily in such matters —and there was even a ludicrous rumour circulated that Coleridge was illicitly connected with Mrs Gillman. And none of these things could Coleridge suffer with any patience, or dignity of indifference.

Again, because he was beyond change, he would spend much time in regretting the past, and it seems as if he was only able to leave his wife topographically. The failure of his marriage is always with him, and he generalises on the marriage state from his own experience of it, in his talk, s. 327 in notes:

The one mighty main defect of female education is that R. 195 everything is taught but reason and the means of retaining affection. This—this—O! it is worth all the rest told ten thousand times:—how to greet a husband, how to receive him, how never to recriminate . . . the love-killing effect of cold, dry, uninterested looks and manners.

Or he turns his non-acceptance of the situation into might-have-been-ism — the sense of unavoidable fate again—I have wasted my talents, he says, and puts down this failure of performance to the prime distraction of his home. "It would have been better for me . . . if I could C. i. 423 have attached more importance, greater warmth of feeling, to my own writings. But I have not been happy enough for that." Hartley, he says, is a poet, "spite of the B. 395 forehead, 'villainously *low*', which his mother smuggled into his face". He cannot get away from the sense of fate, which is strangely supported, he believes, when years later he meets the Mary Evans of old days, now as tragically married, and fixed in as complete a misalliance as himself. C. i. 409

The "fate" is the inability of Coleridge to transcend his

character. The problem is the problem of this character, wherein that which was given to him with one hand was taken away with the other. The strange duality in which unequalled knowledge of the real problems of life, unequalled knowledge of self, was accompanied by the inability to make that knowledge effective in the world of action. All of which Coleridge knows, as he knows every process of his own evolution, and writes down secretly, concealing the words in the wilderness of his haphazard

M. scribblings: "One human being, *entirely* loving me (this, of course, must have been a woman), would not have satisfied all my hopes, but would have rendered me happy and grateful even tho' I had no friend on earth, herself excepted." Then the reason:

M. Doubtless, the fault must have been partly, perhaps chiefly, in myself. The want of reliability in little things . . . the trifling with hope . . . in part to my voluntary self-humiliation, my habitual abasement of myself and talents in comparison with the merits of my friend . . . to the not asserting, and maintaining a greater equality of character . . .

Then the last word:

Unhappy I—I have loved many more than I ever loved myself, and one beyond myself and beyond all things, and all persons, but never, never, have I met with any being who did not love many better than they loved me.

I had forgotten that the last word in this history should come from Mrs Coleridge. In 1822, with her daughter, she visited Highgate. She gives no detail of these meetings, but they have, she says, "been productive of the greatest satisfaction to all parties". A happier note.

I have dwelt on the marriage because whether the letters speak directly of Coleridge or not, the fact of its failure always predominates. In later life Mrs Coleridge's character simplified still further. The reason for her reiterated complaints to Poole of the privations of a deserted wife have little to do with her want of money. Recent editors I. ii. 102, C. prove that Coleridge denied himself to give her what he could, and she was surrounded by helpful friends. "Cole- V. ridge never deserted his wife and children in the sense which the words imply." The real cause of the grievance is that all her pleasures and ambitions—her ethic of prudence and respectability ("'Tis a glorious thing to have a bishop for an uncle")—all centre on the words Family and Home. The regular endings to her letters— when she runs through the short list of Poole's friends with perfunctory enquiry after their health—are meant to offset the half-consciousness that her "egotistical scrawl" has dealt exclusively with her own relations. And everyone will see the contentment beneath the tone of complaint when she records the sicknesses of these relatives, and the minor accidents of their lives, even if it is only Southey's Hay Fever. For Mrs Coleridge, Greta Hall was a kind of family paradise, where she was surrounded by her own children; her sister Mrs Lovell (whose husband, the Pantisocrat, had died in 1796) and her child; her sister Edith, and *her*, very numerous, children; her "brother" Southey (Edith's husband, but no nonsense about "in-laws" for Mrs Coleridge); and a floating population of more distant relations, and friends of relations. The visitors also were welcome, provided they kept clear of the business of the family, but to the family even Friendship, even Art, was subordinate. *Cf.* her strictures on the visit- 19 ing artist who was unfortunate enough, in his efforts to paint a picture, 9 ft. by 8½, of a Woman taking her Infant from an Eagle's Nest to get in the way of one of Mrs Southey's confinements. One can understand the earlier

Fricker instinct to make a kind of matriarchy out of Pantisocracy.

Hartley Coleridge, then, who is prominent in the later pages of this book, appears exclusively as a son. In the Rev. G. H. B. Coleridge's collection of Mrs Coleridge's letters, which exceeds this in bulk, I found that fifty per cent of the numerous letters to Hartley were concerned with the size of his shirts, or the question—when Hartley was already well on in the thirties—whether his clothes were warm enough. In the letters to Poole, the references are less purely maternal. The dramatic, the strictly tragic, elements in his career are illustrated. There is nothing of Hartley as his father early described him, as "A little child, a limber elf, Singing, dancing to itself", or of the boy of ten, struggling with original sin, whom his father B. 514 advised "not to stand between the half-opened door when speaking, or spoken to, but to come *in* or go out", and to whom he refrained from speaking about "mad passions, frantic looks, and pout-mouthing", because he trusted they were all over. Mrs Coleridge's rising pride in her son is shown in letter 7, where she smiles but does not laugh at the friend who says he is sure Hartley is a genius from his manner of opening his mouth, and where she describes the happiness, popularity, and confidence of his mid-teens (in spite of procrastinating ways reminiscent of an ancestor). Then there is the hazardous business of collecting exhibitions, postmasterships, and contributions to allow him to be sent to Merton. Then, the happiest and proudest letter of the whole volume (letter 17) with the news that Hartley is elected Probationary Fellow of Oriel. In the end, when everything ends tragically, when Hartley fails to satisfy in the probationary period, when, because he is disappointed in his attempts to win the Newdigate Prize, or disappointed in love (believing that women despised his shortness, or his awkward manners)—when, for whatever clinical impediment or deficiency in soul Hartley collapses, and allows himself to decay into eccentricities, to become a "character", to go unshaven, and to be found drunk in the gutter by the dean of his College,—then his mother collapses also. She feels herself haunted by the fatal unrespectability of the Coleridges, and it is too much for her. She cannot keep back her tendency to recriminate. The rest of the references to Hartley are mortified and ominous—but much can be learnt of his later diffidence, of how he wandered more mysteriously even than his father "a stranger and a visitor in this world", flitting from unfinished opus to unfinished opus, and demonstrating a fascinating tendency to inherit the human genes from his father to the almost, but not quite, total exclusion of the superhuman ones.

The nearest approach to respectability in Mrs Coleridge's immediate family seems to have been her son Derwent, but next to the career of Hartley, the health of her daughter Sara appears to have absorbed her most. This younger Sara is not so famous now as she was in the nineteenth century, when Dr Garnett said that among female writers she was second only to George Eliot. She was the beauty of the house— "at seventeen, when I last K. 128 saw her, she was the most perfect of all pensive, nun-like, intellectual beauties that I have seen in real breathing life". "Kind Mr de Q." says this—but it is no kind of an exaggeration. Scott thought her a "lovely vision of a O. ii. 342 creature . . . the very ideal of a novel heroine". Nor does her mother exaggerate her abilities. She was one of the delicate, accomplished, literary women of her period— Poole's niece, later Mrs Sandford, and the "Miss E. Poole" of these letters, was another. She appears here before her success, before her novel *Phantasmion*, or *Pretty Lessons in Verse*. She is struggling with her first work, written partly to help with the expenses of Derwent's education—a translation, from Jesuit Latin, of Martin Dobrizhoffer's "Account of the Abipones". Charles Lamb

w. 645 could not bear to think of anyone so beautiful "toiling through five octavos of that cursed . . . Abbeypony His-
w. 740 tory" and wonders how she managed to "Dobrizhoffer it all out". "Heaven send", he added, "that her Uncle do not breed her up a Quarterly Reviewer." Marriage was to save her, for a time. Sara became engaged to H. N. Coleridge, and there is more news for Mr Poole.

Greta Hall is beginning to empty. The last of Southey's children have grown up, and the house has become quieter. Mrs Coleridge is almost lonely again, and shows a pathetic anxiety at the persistence of Sara's lover, and cheerfully prophecies, that for lack of means, there will be "nothing for the young couple now but patience". The marriage when it does come, in 1829, is only made tolerable by the fact that her daughter is marrying a Coleridge, and a cousin. Sara leaves Keswick, and not long after Mrs Coleridge leaves also: but the letters to Poole continue, even without the excuse of news from Greta Hall. Poole still stands, in her mind, for Stowey, for happiness, and the time when she was really a wife, when the family was all her own, and her "sweet Berkeley", who died full thirty years ago, was still alive.

THE 42 LETTERS

1

To M^r. Thos. Poole, Stowey near Bridgewater
Monday Noon. [11th *February*, 1799]

Oh! my dear Mr Poole, I have lost my dear dear child!
at one o'clock on Sunday Morning a violent convulsive
fit put an end to his painful existance, myself and two of
his aunts were watching by his cradle. I wish I had not
seen it, for I am sure it will never leave my memory;
sweet babe! what will thy Father feel when he shall hear
of thy sufferings and death! I am perfectly aware of every
thing you have said on the subject in your letter; I shall
not yet write to Coleridge, and when I do—I will pass over
all disagreeable subjects with the greatest care, for I well
know their violent effect on him—but I account myself
most unfortunate in being at a distance from him at this
time, wanting his consolation as I do, and feeling my
griefs almost too much to support with fortitude. Hartley
is better—but still a little feverish towards evening—he is
taking some cool physic and I mean to have him carried
out every fine day. Southey has undertaken the business
of my babe's interment and in a few days we shall remove
to his house at Westbury which I shall be rejoiced to do
for this house at present is quite hateful to me.

I thank you for the kind letters you sent me and depend
on your writing again—I suppose you will have received
from Coleridge the promised letter for me. I long for it—
for I am very miserable!!!

I wish we were not at such a distance from you and

dear Mrs Poole—you will come to Bristol on the first of March I hope; I shall be tranquil by that time if no other misfortune should happen in the interim and I shall be enabled to meet you with the smile of resignation.

I shall go and see Mrs King when I return from Westbury, perhaps she is now at Stowey.

My money is nearly gone; could you supply me untill Samuel makes me some provision?—I do not chuse to be obliged to any one here—perhaps he may think I have enough to last untill his return not knowing my situation. —I suppose we must direct to C—— at Gottengen.

Please to remember me most kindly to Mrs Poole— God bless her and you and yours

SARA COLERIDGE

My kind respects to Mr Ward; I shall be much obliged to him if he would parcell up the news-papers for me and send them next week by Milton with (I hope) a letter from Coleridge and one from you.

2

Bristol [*March* 1799]

My dear Mr Poole

I am induced to trouble you with a few lines at this time, lest thinking I am gone to Knutsford you might omit sending me the copy of your letter to Samuel, which if you now think proper to do, I shall be here, and happy to recieve it on Thursday by Milton— after which, I will write immediately to him.

By what I could percieve by Mr Ward's manner on Sunday I judge my intended visit to M^{rs} K—— had been a subject of disapprobation to some persons. "*Mrs Poole approves* of your going" said he, "for I suppose you will be no great expence to them"—"certainly not—but she very earnestly invites me to come, and I think I shall accept it"—but upon reflection I shall not and have this evening written to them to be excused. I hope she will not take it amiss—and think me capricious —the idea of expence to them had never occured to me—for I knew that they had four or five hundred pounds a year!

I hope S. T. C. will keep his promise of being with us the first of May—as nearly as he can, and I hope we shall shortly recieve a letter of a later date, for the 14th of Feb. is an age ago.

I do not wonder that you were vexed about the estate— it was very untoward—I wish you may write me word that it is recoverable.

I hope also to hear a continuation of good news of your Mother, Coleridge will be delighted. My very kind love to her and my hearty congratulations. I thank God I am much better than when I last wrote—but still labouring under misfortune—for my poor Mother has thrown a barrel on her foot and bruised it in such a manner that she cannot move out of her Chair— Nanny is no better—and I am without any kind of assistance—with my Mother and the Child to wait on, so that I am as much confined as ever—I am in quest of a Servant.

I am almost ashamed always to write to you in strains of complaint but I expect you to pity and forgive me.

S. C.

The Lyrical Ballads are laughed at and disliked by all with very few excepted.

3

2nd April, 1799

Dr Mr Poole

Your last letter was by neglect of the carrier kept back a week, so that I recd yours for Samuel first— it consequently came too late for me to re-resolve upon a visit to Mrs K. which I regret, for I had set my heart upon it; she has written me a very kind letter still urging me to be her visitor in very affectionate terms; but I now wish to be at Stowey—and should set out very shortly if Nanny were able to accompany me, as it is I know not what to do whether to look out here for a Servant or wait untill I am in the Country, for Nanny I fear will not be able to come at all. Your account of your Mother gave very great pleasure—I hope she will continue to mend untill she is quite well.—My poor Samuel seems to be quite tired of that place, yet says nothing in his last letter of returning but I shall continue to expect him in May, but I suppose it will be the end of it rather than the beginning—I pray to God that nothing may keep him later! For I am weary of this long long absence! I am shocked at the description he gives of the jovial parties, their manners and their Mirth must be excessively disgusting, I wonder how

Chester likes them. My principal reason for troubling now, is to beg you will send me ten Guineas, for I expected Coleridge would have thought of it, but he has not probably thinking I can do without untill he arrives.

I am afraid I shall find the house exceedingly damp—for this reason I have written a few lines to Mrs Rich to beg she will look into it a little and open the windows on fine days.

I shall want the cash as soon as you can provide me with it conveniently for I have many little bills to pay—and I must purchase a few things to bring with me to Stowey; I shall write again before I come home. Hartley is quite well—my Mother is better. But my brother has not been heard of! Please to give very kind love to dear Mrs Poole, my love to Nord—the ladies at the Farm when you see them, and the family at Castle-hill.

God bless you!

SARA COLERIDGE

Thursday, Maudlin Street.

I have been for this week past on a visit at M^r· William Courts! I have been at Bath with them—at the play, concert &c &c and become quite dissipated: but I am now tired—I go to Westbury next week.

Mrs COLERIDGE No 17 Newfoundland St.

The Lyrical Ballads are not liked at all by any.

I have rec^d a very kind invitation to Ottery in .. [?] .. from Mrs G. Coleridge.

It is very unpleasant to me to be often asked if Coleridge has changed his political sentiments—for I know not properly how to reply—pray furnish me.

5

4

College-Street, [Bristol] Thursday Morning [June, 1807]

My dear Sir,

Our intention of paying our respects to you at Stowey on Tuesday evening has been most provokingly frustrated, by a variety of causes—first, Coleridge was so ill on Tuesday morning that he could not rise, on Wednesday the same and this Morning I find some business of his friend Wade's prevents his setting off, he is himself unwell and one of the children poorly, a little feverish & languid;—it is his, and my present intention to leave Bristol to-morrow i.e. Friday morning but as it is utterly impossible for *me* to guess what that morning may produce (*near* although it is) that I write to request you, dear Sir, to pardon this want of punctuality, which believe me is not to [be] reckoned among my numerous faults.—I have had all our Clothes packed since Tuesday, and am waiting with great seeming patience to set off, yet it is my private opinion that we may [not] get off even to-morrow. I am well aware that this letter will not reach you until you have been 4 days in expectation of us, and I wish I had written on Tuesday after my first disappointment, to have saved you at least one day of expectation which I have so often smarted under; but relying on your goodness—with most ardent wishes to see you, (which by the way I hoped to have done long since at Keswick) I remain yours with
much respect, and
affection
S. COLERIDGE

6

It is possible that this letter may reach you not many hours before you see us, as I imagine you will not get this until Friday night.

5

Keswick 28 *December* 1807

My dear Sir,

If Coleridge has not written to you lately, I guess, from the interest you have always taken in our concerns, you will not consider a few lines, even from my feeble pen, an unpardonable intrusion.—But where shall I begin?—I cannot endure to pre-suppose your never having heard anything of us, since C. left your most hospitable dwelling; yet, what is more likely?—However, when he at length joined us at Bristol, in such excellent health, and improved looks, I thought of days "lang sine" and hoped, and prayed it might continue; Alas, in 3 or 4 days it was all over! he said he must go to Town *immediately* about the Lectures, yet he staid 3 weeks without another word about removing, and I durst not speak lest it should *disarrange* him.

Mr de Quincey, who was a frequent visitor to C. in College St., proposed accompanying me and the children into Cumberland, as he wished much to pay Wordsworth and Southey a visit; this was a pleasant scheme for me, only I was obliged to give up my visits in Birm., and Liverpool, which I was rather loth to do, but it was a small evil when set against the great convenience of travelling all the way in Chaises, and under the protecting wing of kind Mr de Q.——

Towards the end of October, I accordingly packed up every thing; C's things (as I thought for London) and our own, and left Bristol towards the end of October; we [reached] Chester on the 3^d night, and the next day got to *Eastham*, and crossed the passage to Liverpool, where we all staid 4 days, and had the pleasure of hearing Madame Catalani sing at the Concert, and afterwards being in her company; she is handsome, and her manner is exceedingly lively and engaging. She passed all her leisure during her stay in L.pool between Lord and Lady Sefton, and the Koster family, [? at] whose house we were during our short stay, only passing one day with the Cromptons, Mr de Q. being in a hurry on account of his being obliged to be at Oxford by the 16th Nov^r—on the second night we all arrived at Grasmere and they wishing us to stay a night, we sent back the Chaise to Ambleside, 3 miles, and ordered it for the next afternoon: they were all in expectation of us at Keswick, and although it was quite dark they had heard the Chaise drive over the Bridge and were out with Lanthorns to light us through the fields, and trying which should get us out first, but Hartley's screams forced Mrs Wilson forward, and he scrambled over bags and baggage to get first to her, we found them all well, and my Sister S. expecting an increase of family. Now for C. I left him (as I thought) ready to jump into the Mail for London, lo! 3 weeks after, I received a letter f^m him dated White-house-stairs Piccadilly, he was just arrived in Town, had been ill, owing to sitting in wet

8

S. T. COLERIDGE

cloathes, and passed 3 weeks at the house of a Mr Morgan, and had been nursed by his wife and her sister in the kindest manner.

C. found Davy very ill: the Lectures on that account were postponed. Stewart had insisted on his being at the Courier Office during his stay in Town; S. always behaves in the most friendly manner to C. yet he never writes to him; Stewart always sends to Keswick when he wishes to gain any intelligence about him. At length Wordsworth obtained a few lines from him, ten days ago—Davy was better, and the Lectures were to commence in a fortnight, since that we have heard nothing.—Dr Stoddart is arrived from Malta, he has brought with him C's papers, C. wrote to him to expostulate with him for having detained them so long; he recieved an abusive answer, saying, "he would deliver up the papers to a person properly documented with 50. pounds for expences &c—C. has since heard that he is writing a Book himself, which accounts for his having kept back the papers; Southey is enraged at his conduct, and foretold this about the Book and gave it as a reason why C.s documents were [not forth]coming; this is rather scandalous, and will do Mas[ter Stoddart's] reputation no good, for independent of his Book [? succee]ding C.'s, it is now much too long after his return to publish a Book about the Mediterranean with much effect.

Have you read the "Travels of Don Manuel Alvarez Espriella?"—I forget whether I mentioned them to you as written by Southey, if I did, do not say so to Southey, as he has only given me leave to mention it *now*: a thousand Copies are in the last hundred, and the second edition in the press; it is rather a popular thing. Southey bids me say that he hopes to pass a couple of days with you in the Spring; he and his Brother Tom leave this place in Feb. for London where Southey will stay a Month, and then travel westward, I shall be cruelly disappointed if you do not fix the time with him for coming to Keswick; and I hope you will stay a great while, for you cannot see the Lakes in a flying visit to any advantage. Tom Southey often talks of the extreme comfort of your house, in which I join most cordially—and the children talk for evermore of the happiness of Stowey.—When you see the Miss Brice's tell them I expect to see them shortly, it is quite the fashion for Gentlemen to bring their *Brides* to the Lakes, and Miss Cruckshank has promised me a visit as soon as she assumes that character, and my Sisters despair of ever coming until they are married, and yet, they give me no hope of seeing them, but perhaps Mr Brice might indulge his daughters with a jaunt, and Mr *Goring* may do a good turn for him.

I am sorry I cannot give you any better account of C. but I hope he has written to you giving an ample account of himself.—He has published a Poem in the Courier lately, "A wanderers farewell" addressed to *two Sisters*, to Mrs Morgan and her Sister. It is a beautiful Poem but it was, in my opinion, a most ungenerous action, the publishing it, it abounds with gratitude to these young Ladies, and bitter complaints and woful murmurings at his own unhappy fate! Southey was sorry that he should do such an unmanly thing as publish such a Poem, and I think his well-wishers must all condemn it. I have never heard the contents of G. C.'s letters, I never could prevail on C. to let me see it. God bless you, my dear Sir, may you be happy as you . . . [?] . . , and think with as much . . . [?] . . . as possible of yours respectfully

S. C.

6

Greta hall, [Keswick] 3rd August, 1810

My dear Sir,

         I hope you will excuse my troubling you with a few lines but I [was] so much disappointed at not seeing you this summer that I cannot resist the great inclination I feel to ask you what has prevented you from performing your promise. Sometime ago my brother had occasion to address a letter to Mr G. Ridout—we hoped we should obtain some tidings of you in that Gentleman's reply but he has not written, and the Autumn is so far advanced I begin to fear you have given up all thoughts of coming to see the North this Year.—S. T. C. has been here the last four or five months, and I am sorry to add that in all that time he has not *appeared* to be employed in composition, although he has repeatedly assured me he was. The last N^o of the "Friend" lies on his Desk, the sight of which fills my heart with grief, and my Eyes with tears; but am obliged to conceal my trouble as much as possible, as the slightest expression of regret never fails to excite resentment—Poor Man!—I have not the least doubt but he is the most unhappy of the two; and the reason is too obvious to need any explanation.—It must,

11

however, be confessed, he has been in almost uniform
kind disposition towards us all during his residence here;
and all Southey's friends who have been here this Summer
have thought his presence a great addition to the society
here; and have all been uniformly great admirers of his
conversation: his spirits too, are in general better than I
have known them for years, and I cannot divine the reason
of his passing his hours in so unprofitable [a] manner.
Yet, I must not say that his abode here has been without
some advantages to us, for as soon as he came, finding
his daughter was desirous of learning Latin, which she had
begun, he thought it a good opportunity of teaching both
her and her Mother the Italian Language while he staid: I
was rejoiced at this offer but was afraid he would not persevere, and I am convinced he would very often have put off
the child, when he could not find an excuse to send us *both*
away when our tasks were ready.—Sara has read through
a little book of Poems in that Language, many of which
she can repeat, and we are now trying the PASTOR FIDO.

In your last you [were] so good as to make particular
enquiries about the boys' Mode of Education &c—M^r
Dawes readily undertook to instruct them in Greek before
Latin, their father promising to supply them with proper
lessons, as he knew not well how to proceed without a
Lexicon.—C. bought them a Parkhurst for the translation
of the Testament but now they are in Homer, poor
fellows, they are obliged to look out in a Latin and Greek
Dictionary which H. grumbled at, at first, but now he
says he is glad of it, for he shall have no trouble whatever
in learning Latin.—Mr Dawes was here in the Mid-

12

summer Vacation and Coleridge & myself and Southey thanked [him] for the care he had taken to improve the children; he modestly said that no merit belonged to him, for they had *both* [such] extraordinary abilities that he thought they ought to be very soon under an abler Master than himself: of course we laughed at this, but at the same time received great pleasure from the account he gave of them.—H. we hear, has a dislike to figures, but Derwent is very far advanced in them. C. hopes he will have a turn for Mathematics, he is to begin Algebra very soon—H. of course is far before his brother in Greek—and he knows a great deal more of Geography than his brother and Mr Dawes says he makes H. his brother's teacher as much as possible. Hartley has just attained his 14th year, he has grown much in the last two years, and he is a great deal stronger than he promised to be when we were with you 3 years ago—Derwent is 10 years old and a little fellow of his Age. My sister has just lain in of her sixth child—they have 4 living, 3 daughters and a Son—the eldest daughter is 14 months younger than *Sara*, but she is full as *tall* and far *heavier*, she has no great "love of books" at present, but we hope *that time* is to come. Sara will be spoilt in being so often quoted to excite the emulation of her idler cousin, who has full as good abilities as herself, but not *yet* so much perseverance. Mr [?] told me wonderful things of your Niece Miss E. P.—I shall be very glad to hear of her when you can afford me a few lines, and of Mrs King & family—Mr Ward & all my Stowey friends & in particular the Riches & Mrs Cole. I was much shocked at the account of poor Blake, but I

think my dear Sir I should feel for many parents more
than for his;—I never could consider them as very affectionate towards him—but the separation & disgrace must
be dreadful, even to them; and I daresay poor M^{rs} &
Mr Cole had their full share in this   misfortune!
My dear Mr P. I am very sorry   conclusion to my
poor letter, but it must be confessed [? that C. must]*
very shortly arouse from his lethargy, our . . . poor condition:—for if I am not greatly . . . involved in difficulties
which nothing . . . will extricate him from; and even
with it I fear it cannot speedily be done for the business
of the "Friend" is managed so wretchedly owing to his
not giving it into the hands of a regular Publisher that I
fear nothing will ever come of it, as far as profit is con-
cerned; even Southey says it is well it was begun because
there is so much got out of him which would never otherwise have come out—heaven knows, I am so bewildered
about our affairs that I know not what to wish or what
to *do*—these Lads too, H. in particular is fast approaching
towards Manhood—what can he think is to become of
them if he does not exert himself—these dear Boys are the
source of much pleasure to me at present—heaven only
knows how long it will last!

A few weeks since I rec^d a short note fm Mr *W[edg-
wood]* saying that I must hereafter leave 10 p^r ct. in the
Banker's hands for the property Tax, this reduces the
annuity to 135 p^r Annum, he says we ought to [have] paid
this long ago: I wished C. . . . answer the Note but could
not prevail. . . .

* MS. obliterated.

14

7

Keswick, October 30. *not sent off until Novem.* 14. [1812]

My dear Sir,

   For the last three months we have looked anxiously for a letter from you, to announce to us your long expected visit: Alas, you have suffered half the Autumn to elapse without signifying any intention of this kind.—Well—perhaps next year will be propitious and if it bring you to us, we will endeavour, in the sincere pleasure we shall feel in bidding you welcome, to forget the pain of repeated disappointments.—

What a kind and deeply interesting letter was your last—I have delayed thanking you for it almost two years in the hope of seeing you and also, with a wish to send you some news of Coleridge that might give you pleasure, to repay you in some measure for intruding upon you; having gained nothing by this delay, I take up my pen in a moment of despair, depending upon your friendly assurances that you will read my letter with some degree of interest, and favour me with a few lines when it shall happen to be convenient to you.—Coleridge has not written to me or any of his Northern friends for three months past, but I hear through Lamb that he has offered his Tragedy to one of the Theatres, and that it is now in Mr Whitbread's hands—he is, no doubt very much pressed for money and *that* has induced him to try his fortune— heaven grant that it succeed, for never were his exertions so absolutely, so imperiously necessary to his family as

at this juncture. You doubtless heard from Southey of
the estrangement of C. from W.—Coleridge came to us
last Feb., took up the Boys at Ambleside, rode through
Grasmere without stopping at Wordsworth's!—Poor
Hartley sat in speachless astonishment as the Chaise
passed the turning to the Vicarage where W. lives, but he
dared not hazard one remark and Derwent fixed his eyes
full of tears upon his father, who turned his head away to
conceal his own emotions—when they had an opportunity they both eagerly asked the meaning of this para-
dox, and H. turned as white, as lime, when I told him that
Mr W. had a little vexed his father by something he had
said to Mr Montagu—which through mistake had been
misrepresented: these children in the habit of going
weekly to Grasmere could not comprehend how these
things were.—Numerous were the letters and messages I
received from Miss W. to urge C. to write to her and not
to leave the country without seeing them; but he would
not go to *them* and *they* did not come to him, so after
staying 6 weeks he returned to give his Lectures at Willis's
rooms—while he was delivering them, W. went to Town,
was present at some of the Lectures with the Beaumonts,
who interested themselves greatly in endeavouring to
bring about a reconciliation between the friends, which
was at last effected through the medium of Mr H. Robin-
son but I think, I may venture to say, there will never
more be *that* between them which was in days of yore—
but it has taught C. one useful lesson; that even his
dearest & most indulgent friends, even those very persons
who have been the great means of his self-indulgence,

16

when he comes to live *wholly* with them, are *as* clear-
sighted to his failings, & much *less* delicate in speaking
of them, than his Wife, who being the Mother of his
children, even if she had not the slightest regard for himself, would naturally feel a reluctance to the exposing of
his faults.

When C. was here in Feb^{ry} he was cheerful & good
natured & full of fair promises—he talked of our setling
finally in London, that is, when he had gone on for a year
or so giving me, and all his friends satisfaction as to the
possibility of making a livelihood by his writings so as to
enable us to live in great credit there—I listened, I own,
with incredulous ears, while he was building these "airy
castles" and calmly told him that I thought it was much
better that I and the children should remain in the country
until the Boys had finished their School-education and
then, if he found himself in circumstances that would
admit of it, & would engage not to leave us all alone in
that wide city, I would cheerfully take leave of *dear
Keswick*, and follow his amended fortunes; he agreed to
this, & in the meantime, a regular correspondence *was* to
be kept up between himself, and me, and the children;
and *never more* was he to keep a letter of mine, or the
Boys', or Southey's *un*opened—his promises, poor fellow,
are like his Castles,—airy nothings!—One only excuse can
I make at this time for his neglect of us, his agitations
about Wordsworth—he has not even written to me since
the reconciliation: I heard it all from Wordsworth himself (being at Grasmere with my daughter & neice while
W. was in London;) & also from Mr Morgan.

—Hartley is now just turned of 16—he is much grown in the last 4 years, and has a voice deeper than his father's, with a great deal of his father's manner—so much so, that Dr Bell, (who has been here lately to our great delight, for we are all much in his favour, and most sincerely attached to *him*, he has just now left Keswick and is gone for a week to Rose-Castle—i.e.—Bish^p Carlisle's) was much amused when he first saw him, and said, he was sure he was a Genius by the manner of opening his Mouth:—his Master speaks in high terms of his powers of mind and habits of Study, but laments his procrastinating ways, and habit of doing *anything* rather than the *right* thing, in the *right* time, *too* much in this respect like a near relation of his, who sees this likeness, and bitterly laments it. H. at present seems to have a decided preference for the Church—else, many persons have thought that his talents would be more useful in the Law—as he has the "Gift of the Gab"—in no small degree, and, notwithstanding what he says of fears & tremblings, a great confidence in speaking.—He is a great favourite in the neighbourhood of his School, and perhaps a little spoilt by being often in the company of people of fashion, where he is not only *permitted*, but *expected* to talk. Little D., now 12 years old, says, Mother, I assure you Hartley is quite spoilt when he is out, people call him "Sir," and treat him like a Man, and that is the reason he is so conceited.—W. however tells me that when he sees him at Rydale Hall—the Seat of L^y Diana Flemming— he never speaks but when he is addressed, and that they both behave with proper modesty; W. has a most friendly

18

regard for these Boys, and an ardent interest in their
future well-doing—and was affected with a very lively
pleasure when I mentioned *that sentence* in your letter
respecting the University, desiring me [to] say how much
he wishes to converse with you on that subject whenever
he may have the happiness to enjoy your society here:—
Southey would have written to you if I had not mentioned
my intention, he begs his best regards to you with mine
& my sisters'; he says he shall account himself very happy
when he can see you under this roof—We have had a
great abundance of company, I think we see more & more
people every year: we have been very full in the house
too, Miss Barker & her servant have been here since midsummer, in search of a house near us; she has succeeded
in getting one close by us, where she is now setling herself.
We have had Mr Danvers Jardine, his ward, & M^r S.
Ried:—& my sister Martha has been here all the summer.
—We have now in the house Mr Dawe & his sister; M^r D.
took a Chalk drawing of C. & a bust last winter; they
were in the exhibition. H & D. are now at home, receiving
instruction in drawing from Miss D. together with Sara,
Edith & Herbert, but *they* (the Boys) must soon return to
School for my sister is on the verge of her seventh
Accouchement, and when they go, we hope Mr D. will
also return to Town for he is painting a great Picture in
C's Study, subject,—"A Woman on the point of a high
Rock, taking her infant from an Eagle's Nest; the Eagle
flying over her head"—and this painting business creates
a great deal of bustle—and running *in* and *out*, windows
open to paint the scenery &c &c—which we can well dis-

pense with in her confinement—the picture is 9 feet by
8½—how it is to travel to Town, I cannot guess.—What
wonders do I hear of your extraordinary Niece!—the
account you give yourself is most interesting—our children must appear mere pigmies in your eyes after her—my
little Girl just remembers the pleasures of your hospitable
dwelling, & wishes to know if she shall ever see it again—
She is an excellent Scholar—& no trouble to teach, her
brothers teach [her] in the holidays, so she picks up a little
knowledge between us all—her father is very good to her
when he is here, & complimented me on her progress in
Italian &c. She can read a little French, and she is learning
Latin, we have no Music yet—

Novr 14. Since writing the above, which I had not the
courage to send off, my sister is brought to Bed of her
sixth daughter; the Dawes have left us, Picture & all, &
the Boys are gone back to school: I have heard from
Martha that C's Play is accepted & he has begun Lec-
turing. Martha left us a few days since in search of a situation in Town, her health & spirits are much injured in her
long confinement with our poor Mother; she was obliged
to neglect her business and at last it was so much decreased
that she gave it up altogether, for she had a house of a
great rent upon her hands which she could not always
lett well. I fear her long visit in this house will give her a
greater distaste to the confinements & mortifications of her
situation than she had before. She is about to enter into
partnership with a Lady in Tichfield Street, & we hear it
will answer. Martha tells that she was at C's second Lecture
[and] that he looked well & spoke with great animation.

Colonel Peachey & his new wife are at the Island; she is a very amiable woman & thought very handsome by most people here, but we cannot yet see half the sweetness in her that at all times we saw in the dear departed—she was a woman in ten thousand! Dr Sir, when you see Mrs King pray remember me most kindly to her; to Mr Ward, also, whom I heartily congratulate on his marriage; although rather late to do it. To all my Stowey friends & those in the neighbourhood I beg to be very kindly remembered; & in the hope of a few lines from your hands when you have a little leisure, containing a promise of some future intention to visit the *Mountain Bards*, I remain ever your obliged

S. COLERIDGE

8

[*Keswick*] [*February*, 1814]

My dear Sir

The desire I feel to hear that you are in health, & that you have not given up your intention of paying us a visit at the Lakes is so importunate that I cannot longer defer troubling you with a few lines to ask if you received a letter from [me] sometime early in the last spring—I think I wrote during the rehearsal of S. T. C.'s play, but having sent it to town to be franked, it is very likely to have miscarried.

Our intelligent neighbour Mr de Quincey tells me, that you had been with Mr C. in London during the last year; you would naturally imagine that he would mention this circumstance to me in his letters—but unhappily for me & the dear children, & I may add, for himself, his aversion to writing of every kind seems to strengthen with every absence—we have not seen him for 2 years—& it will be 12 Months in March since he wrote to Keswick—having only sent me one letter during 2 years.—When my brother Southey returned from London, C. promised to accompany him; we were all sadly disappointed when the Chaise arrived with only *one* person in it—S. however assured us, that he would be here shortly, having gone to Bristol to deliver a course of Lectures, after which he would set off for Keswick to meet the Boys at the Christmas holidays—so I kept them at home in the hope of a letter giving some direction about Hartley's studies, but none coming, I sent the poor fellows back last Monday, with their Skaits across their shoulders; Derwent who is a very *Keen* Skaiter, casting many a ling'ring look behind upon our frozen Lake, and praying for a Snowstorm to drive him back again. His brother, on the contrary, marched back with cheerful feet, knowing he is only to stay at that School until his father comes—he wished to go back as soon as possible to be with Mr Dawes, whom he both loves & respects in a very high degree. As H. is now turned of 17 I think I should not have sent [him] back to school at all, if it had not been for his very great desire to return—and among the many reasons he gave for it— *one* was, that he could not study Euclid so well without the assistance of his brother, who is much beyond him in this branch of science.—He has left a letter for a young friend to be sealed & to go by private hand; I take the

liberty of sending you an *extract* from it—it is written to
a boy of his own age who is at one of those expensive
seminaries, where they take only 4 pupils—but I do not
think he is a much better *classic* than H. at present, he is,
however, in a good train to prepare himself for the
university.—

"I do not wonder that you find Homer *less* difficult
than you expected; there is nothing really difficult in him,
except the dialects, and those, with little attention, one
soon gets master of—Virgil too, is very easy, but Terence
has, (as far as I am enabled to judge,) all the difficulties
that must attend a writer of Comedy. Besides Homer &
Virgil, I read in Greek, Epictetus, (a stoic phlopher, whose
precepts are easier to *construe*, than to *practice*,) &
Æschylus—Xenophon I have not looked at for some time
past—in Latin, Livy's R. H., the only difficulty of which
is, in finding good english phrases correspondent to the
Latin ones, for the meaning is generally obvious enough—
the subject is deeply interesting, but the minuteness of the
Author in describing customs, ceremonies, Omens, pro-
digies &c. is to me, I confess, somewhat tedious. The latin
of the historians, (those that I have hitherto seen) is much
more remote from English than that of the Poets—Caesar
is, however, an exception to this. Cicero's orations are the
finest latin compositions I have seen, at least in prose:
Have you written much latin yet? that is rather a troublesome task to me at present, especially in verse,—I have
only lately applied myself to it, I shall be glad to know
what progress you make.—I have now, I am happy to
say, got clear of the shoals of Arithmetic,—and am

launching out into the wide sea of Mathematics; though
I shall be able to give but a bad account of my voyage,
the weather has been so intolerably foggy. However, I
have stumbled over about half of Bonnycastle's Mensura-
tion, I study or ought to study Euclid's elements—& here
I cannot but mention Derwent's good progress in this
science — he perfectly understands, & has in a great
measure, committed to memory, *two* or *three* books of
Euclid's Geometry—which is his favorite study—tho' he
is not deficient in any other, & I have no doubt that my
father at his return, will be well satisfied with him, whenever that much wished-for event arrives."

—I suppose you have heard of the death of my poor
brother—if I rightly remember, he had just come to
Keswick when I last addressed you; it was a great comfort to us that he should be under this roof in his last sickness, for he would have been very differently nursed, poor
fellow, if he had remained at Bristol where he has no
relations left, except one good, kind family, (the Perkins's)
who would not have been able to have watched him night
and day through a long sickness—never was there a more
patient sufferer than he was!—my sister Eliza arrived a
fortnight before his death—it was a mournful meeting,
for he was nothing but skin and bone—he grew so rapidly
thin, after the rupture of the blood vessel—she was a
great comfort to him—for she was his favorite sister having been children, and *playmates* together—he lies in
Keswick Church-yard, near Mr Jackson—& the little dear
Emma Southey—and we all greatly fear *another* will
shortly lie beside them, from this hill.—you must remem-

ber Basil Montagu a little boy at Allfoxden, he lies
dangerously ill at the house of our friend Miss Barker
next door to us—to whose house he came from Ambleside 5 weeks ago—for a visit of a few days; he has been
at sea for the last 7 years, & being in ill health his father
sent him to Ambleside to a lodging there for a little
recreation:—the day after his arrival at Keswick he was
sitting in Southey's study, he began violently to vomit
blood, and hearing a bustle up stairs, we (—i.e. myself
and sisters) ran up—*think*, what must be our astonishment
& grief—when looking into the chamber, we saw this
poor youth, in the same attitude, dress and much the
same figure—with Southey hanging anxiously over him,
just as a few months before we had seen poor George,
bringing up streams of blood from the lungs—it was a
most striking co-incidence—never to be forgotten!—
Southey & the surgeon supported him across the garden
to his bed at Miss B's, where he has lain almost ever since,
bleeding 2 or 3 times in the 24 hours, until the last week,
when he sat up a little—but *now* he has a violent pain in
his side—is *blistered* and *again bled* in the Arm, and cannot get out of bed but for a few minutes with the help of
Miss B's boy and the Surgeon—and Miss Wordsworth
tells us to-day that she sees no prospect whatever of his
removal—Miss B—— & Miss W. take [it] by turns to
watch his bed side, & sometimes they are assisted by an
old servant of Miss B's—— I have not been able to be of
much use to them, for we have had a very sick house—
little Edith has had the scarlet fever—Derwent has had a
sickness since B. M. has been here—and my poor little

25

Sara strained her heel some months ago—having danced
a good deal in the beginning of the Xmas holidays she
made it so much worse that she is obliged to have a
blister & .. [?] .. the pain is oftentimes so tedious that I
am obliged to sit up in the bed and rub [for] a considerable
time, so that she cannot be left at night—she is also quite
langu[id and] her appetite and spirits have forsaken her
—we must have recourse to some [?] Port wine to give
her wonted elasticity—poor little love! She is but a tender
creature and because she is rather forwarder in her books
than most of the little Girls around us—the *wise* Mamas,
forsooth, insist upon it, that she is killed with study—but
although she is fond of improvement—she is far *fonder* of
play, and as to *work*, she will not set a stitch unless it be
fancywork.—Our kind friend, Mrs Calvert wife of one [of]
our magistrates—was so *certain* last summer that Sara
wanted to get away from her books that she persuaded me
to lett her go with her and her family to the [Sea to]
bathe—she went—and certainly came back looking a good
deal fresher—the Sea-air and bathing is an excellent thing,
to people who want bracing—and if it were not for the
expence, I should be glad to go thither with D & S. next
spring.—I need not repeat, dear Sir, how grateful I should
be for a few lines from you, when you have a quarter of
an hour to spare—and to see you here will be a pleasure
indeed.—Tell me, I beseech you, something of Miss E.
Poole—who must be now near 14 years of age—you
know *how* I am so well acquainted with her age—my
dearest Berkeley!—I have no more anxieties about thee!
—Remember me most kindly to my friend Mr Ward—I

hear he is married, has he any family? is Miss Brice married?—or Miss M. Cruckshank—I beg to be kindly remembered when you see them to Mrs Cole—M^rs R; and Betty Reynal, & all my kind Stowey friends whom I remember with a grateful pleasure!—We have no increase of the Southey family since I wrote: 4 Girls and a dear boy is their present number—& I cannot say I am at all anxious for an addition to it—for indeed we are a house *quite* full when we are altogether—at Christmas we seemed like bees in a Hive—for now Eliza is here we are 4 women —Southey—8 children 3 servants—& Hartley thought we were not quite thick enough—so he sends for a youth of his own age to come and Scait upon *Derwent-water*—he staid a fortnight—and at the same time Miss Barker had little Dorothy Wordsworth & another young lady at her house, who were half the time here but the other half— indeed, we got rid of half a dozen of them when they were altogether in at Miss B's—she was so kind as to give them a Ball on new year's-day.—When my sister Eliza left B. last summer I desired her to call on Mrs King in my name to enquire of the health of herself & family; I was sorry to learn from her that you had been afflicted with the Gout—I sincerely hope you have had no return of that severe disorder.—Mr Wordsworth's family is now reduced to 3 children. I suppose you know that he has an appointment to the office of Stamp-distributor to the 2 Counties—& my brother's (Southey's) Laurels are doubtless well known to you—and you also know, that unlike Mr Wordsworth's place—it is more *honour* than *profit*— Wordsworth keeps a sort of secretary to do the drudgery

27

of the office, and to travel for it.—I have said but little
of S. T. C. because I think it likely enough, that you have
either seen him at Bristol—or heard of him from M^{rs}
King—Southey writes to Danvers—and from him we
learn that Coleridge has been very ill—but is better &
intends coming soon—if he does not shortly *recollect* that
he has a *wife & three children* in the *north* of England,
who can *now*, *less than ever*, do without his pecuniary
aid—I believe they must all travel *south* and join him &
try their fortune together—Ah my dear Sir,—Mr Wedge-
wood, I daresay, little guesses the *increase of anxieties* his
withdrawing his half of the annuity has caused me—but
it was not to be expected that he could be interested about
those whom he had never seen—I think if [he] *had* ever
seen these children, he would not have had the heart to
have withdrawn it—at least until one of them was in a
way of providing for himself—but I blame *nobody*—and
these *murmurs* of an oppressed heart, are only for the
ears of an indulgent friend—this much more—and I have
done—if it were not for the protection that Southey's
house affords me—I know not how we should [*all* have
gone on] at this present writing—I remain however in
much trouble yet thankful for the *blessings* remaining to
me—(I need not name them) and in hope of better pros-
pects or C's return even, dear Mr Poole, yours very
sincerely

S. C.

——on looking over what I have written, I cannot but
feel it necessary to apologize to you for dwelling so much
upon trifles—pray pardon me—excuse the many blunders

I have committed, owing to my agitation of spirits in part
—and to my writing in a room full of Children—for we
keep regular School from ½ past nine until 4 with the
exception of an hour for walking and an half hour for
dressing—Mrs Lovel keeps school in a small room for
English and Latin—and the writing and figures—french
—italian &c are done with me in the *dining room* with
the assistance of Aunt Eliza—and Southey teaches
his wife and daughters to read spanish in the . . ? . . and
his son Greek—should we not all be very learned!
—At Miss Barkers are displayed accomplishments
of a different kind—she is a proficient in drawing—
plays pretty well at the Harp & Harpsichord—& is
(between ourselves) a bit of a poetess—now I give you
full leave to laugh at this pompous description of
our occupations—& assure you that if you will . . ? . .

9

Greta hall January 2^d 1815.

My dear Sir.

   I have waited a long time in the hope of
hearing some news, either *of* or *from* Mr Coleridge, before
I addressed a few lines to you to thank you for your kind
promise, with respect to my Son Hartley; & to inform
you of what has been done by our other kind friends to
enable him to finish his education at Oxford. My brother
Southey wrote a statement of our situation to M^r G.
Coleridge, who promised to try, through his nephews, to

get some exhibition at one of the Colleges for this "father-
less child" (as he affectingly termed him) and engaged to
allow him £40 a year—I think he said *we* will do this, but
I do not know which of the brothers (he means, beside
himself) which with £30 from Lady Beaumont, and your
£10, make £80 per Annum—but that unless they could
raise a hundred & thirty he thought he could not be
supported there.

Since this letter he has sent us one from his Nephew
the revᵈ Wᵐ Coleridge, who has obtained a promise of a
Postmastership at Merton College for his cousin, the
privileges of which will amount to near £50 pounds a
year—such as a free table for dinner, so much per Month
from the Buttery—which is equal to breakfasts—and
money for certain ..?.. given at holydays which will
amount to near fifty according to William's calculation,
if so, he will have equal to £130 a year, which with the
strictest management may suffice. One thing he mentioned as rather a *drawback*, was, that he will always be
expected to leave College at Vacations; and as his HOME,
poor fellow, is so distant (I have bitter feelings attached
to the word HOME) that it will be expensive to reach it at
every vacation: but if possible he *should* come to the
North during the long Autumn Vacation; and the shorter
ones he must pass with his southern friends, from several
of whom he has had invitations, but unfortunately they
mostly live remote from Oxford, however, as he is a
capital walker, he may manage to save expence by walking to any moderate distance.—The *"extract"* sent us
from Wᵐ C[oleridge]'s letter, was very honorable to him,

—he concludes by saying—"I think we have been very fortunate in getting *this* for Hartley—and I will do all I can to assist him, having no money to offer I will do all I can in giving my *time*, lending him books—and rendering him all the assistance in my power; and as I shall be at College, I can sometimes manage for him about not *always* quitting College." (I suppose the *reason* for the *necessity* of *quitting*, is on account of the *free table*, I can divine no other)

General Peachey tells me, that a *Postmastership* at Merton is the same thing as a *Scholarship* in other Colleges—with this exception, that it ceases in 4 years,—but we hope in four years he will be advancing towards a fellowship—his cousins John & W^m are both fellows. Perhaps you will be a little surprised at not seeing his cousin John, who is the cleverest of the Coleridge's, associated in the endeavour to get something for H. at the university, the reason is, that he was at Geneva at the time the application was made, or I have little doubt, that his interest would have been exerted.—I believe he is to go at Easter, and in the meantime his Uncle G. C. recommends him to pay great attention to Latin, & get perfect, at least, the six first Books of Euclid. H. has left School since last June, but he studies pretty hard at home; he has been for the last month, on a *visit* to Mr Dawes,— and attends the School every morning—I expect him home this day.—I believe dear Sir, I have mentioned every needful particular, relative to this business which you are so good as to interest yourself in, and before I conclude I must mention the great kindness and solicitude we have experienced from Wordsworth & his family respecting an unfortunate situation, with promises of assistance &c.—and to Southey I am in every manner everlastingly bound: I pray heaven to reward you all, for yr. goodness!—You will be shocked to hear that I never hear from C. I dare not dwell upon the painful consequences of his desertion but if in the Spring he does not exert himself to pay some of my debts here—I really do not know what will be the result.—The poor children, are miserable if their father is mentioned for fear they should hear anything like blame attached to it, but I believe I mentioned to you before their great sensibility on this unhappy subject.—You will be pleased, however, to hear, that Sara has recovered the use of her foot, now intirely, and is, (as far as one so delicate, can be) in perfect health.

The second Edition of S's Roderick is in the press—I have not heard how the "Excursion" goes off; nor have I yet, seen any *review* of it; but I guess what will be the tone of the Edinburgh. I was much surprised, one morning, by a visit from M^{rs} M'Taggart whom I had never seen since the lifetime of my sweet Berkeley; I felt a melancholy pleasure in looking at her, because she had once sat, for a considerable time in silence, by that Infant's cradle, contemplating him, I supposed, with admiration; and because he was beloved by yr. dear mother.

*   *   *

10

Greta hall March 28*th* 1815

My dear Sir,

   I received your kind letter last night rather too late to write by the Post having dined out; accept our united thanks for it, and the enclosed.

You are very good to write to me so many particulars respecting my old friends at Stowey, for whom I shall always feel interested and am sorry to hear such bad accounts of the Cruckshank family; that inordinate love of show & expence seems to infect every individual of it; yet there must be much good about them or you, who disapprove so decidedly, of this species of folly would not continue to interest yourself so much about them; I sincerely wish them freedom from their embarrasments.— We have just received a letter from Mr C.'s friend Mr Morgan of Calne in Wilts. He says he is not intirely without hope that C. will do something now for his family, as he is now in good health & spirits, & talks of beginning in good earnest a German translation which will be profitable and which Mr M. kindly promises to take all the fag of, & only require the business of correction from C. which will leave him at liberty to get his Poems ready for the press; he says he has been at Devises, Corsham, on visits, and Bath, & at each place got ill, and here he says, he is far too much in company, but nothing shall be wanting on his part to be of use, and to keep him in health. I am afraid, he has still his old habit of swallowing Opium, & if he continue in it, I fear no good will ever come from him.

On the second of May it is my intention, (if we live as long, and Providence permit) to go to Rydal-Mount with H. & Sara, and on the 8th H. must take leave of his most dear northern friends, & shaking off all childish habits, sett forward to meet his new found relation Wm C. who promises, in his several letters to us, not only to consider him as his cousin, but as a Pupil also, for whom he shall exert himself in no common manner, "for we," he says, "expect great things of my cousin H. and we hear that he is a youth of very amiable dispositions, & those little peculiarities of manner, which from the nature of his education he may have contracted, will soon wear away when he is fairly setled amongst us."—Poor fellow, he wishes they had never heard anything of him beforehand, for he is afraid he shall be found sadly wanting, when the time comes; "and I know I shall be laughed at, for I always have been so, but the laugh I have hitherto encountered has had no *scorn* or *bitterness* in it, but I shall go pretty well prepared to meet the scoffs and ridicule of the unfeeling, in the full assurance that in the [? greater] number, I shall, as I have hitherto done, meet with kind consideration."—Heaven grant it may prove so!—One thing, however, I have warned him against, that of flying about in the open air, and uttering his poetic fancies aloud: this he constantly does, when the fit is on him, whether it rain or shine, whether it be dark or light, and when we are sitting in the Parlour with the Curtains drawn, between the whistling of the wind, we hear him whizzing by, and sometimes his Uncle calls out to him "whither so fast Endymion?" alluding to his visits at Rydal-hall to Lady Diana Flemming, who is an old Lady, & about whom poor H. cannot endure to be teized. Derwent, whom you are so good as to mention, is better than he was in the winter, and is at his old School at Ambleside, which he likes well, all *but* for *one reason*, he wants to be forwarded in Algebra & all the branches of Mathematics, which are not attended to under Mr Dawes.—I have indeed, [as] you truly say, most uncommon friends in both the Gentlemen you mention, they are good to every body that comes within their sphere; I think you will like their recent publications when you read them. "Roderick" is to me the pleasan[test] of all S's poetical works.

You say nothing of the public news, Alas what can be said? One thing however we have reason to be thankful for, that we have no dear friends now in Paris, for if it had happen[ed] later, Miss B—— Miss Hutchinson and Miss Barker would have been there; they meant to go in May. Poor M^{rs} M'Taggart, we are extremely sorry to hear of her misfortune. God bless you, my dear Sir, and all good

> ever more your truly obliged
>
> S. COLERIDGE

Sara begs her kind remembrances to you, she thinks she has a faint recollection of your person; & that you used to call her funny.

11

Keswick 20 *September* [1815]

I wish my dear Sir I could be quite sure that a few lines from me at this time would not be troublesome to you, I should, in that case, send a few lines with a greater degree of confidence. Be assured, however, that I am far from expecting you to write in return, unless you have anything particular to communicate; but I thought you might (if you have not heard through any other channel,) be pleased to hear something respecting us, & particularly of Hartley's commencement at Oxford.

I believe you were informed by Mr Wordsworth, that Mr Wm Coleridge, fellow of Ch. Ch., had produced a Postmastership for H. at Merton; fortunately he & Mr W. were going southward just at the commencement of the term; they took him to Oxford, where they were delighted with the reception they all received from W. C. who promised to make H. acquainted with all things needful, & to give him every possible assistance; they left Oxford the next day for London, & I received pleasing accounts from H. during his stay of six weeks only, when he left O: for Mr Morgan's residence at Calne, Wilts., where I receive frequent letters from him; he returns to College in October.—Coleridge, it appears, has sent 2 vols: to the press; a republication of the former poems, with others, & a literary life of the Author, which has grown out of the preface; & is, if we may believe his son, an interesting part of the work: it is printing at Bristol

but is to be, I suppose, published in London.—Heaven
knows I have great reason to pray for its success, but it
appears to me that Mr Morgan is too sanguine when he
hopes C. will get some hundreds for this publication.
How do you like Wordsworth's *"Excursion"* & *"The
white Doe"*? there are still *two* very opposite opinions
concerning his poetry, you know ours, & Sir George &
Lady Beaumont (who have just quitted K. for Lowther,
seat of the Earl of Lonsdale,) think him the finest of
literary poets. "Roderick" has had a rapid sale, and is, I
believe pretty popular. S. is printing his 2 vol: hist:
Brazil. We have had for 2 months on a visit here a Son of
Mr Koster of L.pool, late Merchant at Lisbon. Southey's
acquaintance commenced with this family at Lisbon when
the Gentleman alluded to was a child, he is now employing himself in translating S. hist. B. into the portuguese
language for the benefit of the Brazilians, among whom
he has resided chiefly since the age of sixteen; he is now
22—& has been in England only 5 months, he with S. &
his wife & eldest daughter left Keswick last Tuesday for
London where they will join Dr Southey & his bride, her
mother & sister, & proceed to Ramsgate—for Flanders—
where they mean to pass some weeks, at Brussels, Water-
loo &c. &c. & afterwards to stay a few weeks in London
so that I shall not see them till the winter has commenced; Mrs Lovell myself & little daughter being left
to amuse ourselves and take care of the son & 3 remaining
daughters of the travellers, whom God preserve, for the
vessel that bears them will have a precious freight; as
beside the Southeys, there is Mr H. Koster a most beloved

Son & brother, whose parents have lost his 2 elder
brothers, both grown up, and are not likely to rear their
only other son—of 12 years, who is in ill health; on his
return he is expected to commence Merchant, much, I
fear against his present inclinations. Dr S. has married a
Miss Louisa Gonne, daughter of the late Mr Gonne,
formerly of Lisbon, Merchant. This Lady must be ten
years younger than her husband, beautifull and in expectation of a very large fortune—she has married certainly
one of the handsomest & best mannered Men in this
kingdom, rising in his profession and of an excellent disposition; he visited Keswick last autumn and we all
thought we should not often look upon his like. M^{rs} G.
is an old Lisbon friend of Edith's, much esteemed by her
& all who know her; she leaves a young family at home
to accompany her daughters on this tour, her married
daughter has been much an invalid for some years. Have
[you] ever heard, my dear Sir, of the rejoicings we have
had on the top of our great mountain Skiddaw, most
likely you have seen an account of it in the papers, of a
bonfire upon the highest summit of that high mountain;
Wordsworth & Southey & their fam[ilies] ascended, beside a very large party of Ladies & gentlemen [among]
whom were Lord & Lady Sunderlin, the former 76 & the
latter upwards of 60 years old—Sir G. Beaumont had
imprudently walked to the summit in the morning, so
could not go at night, so he, with his Lady—and the
Misses Malone, with a great many others were content to
review the sight from our windows, and a splendid thing
it was to behold, and seeing the company descend the

hill by the light of Torches had a most uncommon &
beautiful effect; they reached the vale at half past 12 at
midnight, after which we sent up a fire balloon and a
number of small fire works. All Mr Dawes's boys came
over from Ambleside, not time enough to ascend the hill,
which vexed poor Derwent much, so that no one of our
Name was there, for I am not equal to a walk of ten
miles mountain road & Sara is much too delicate to be
permitted such a thing. She saw her cousins—Edith &
Herbert—set out with tears in her eyes, protesting she
could perform the thing with the greatest ease, but all set
a face against her attempting it—I had a very anxious
time during the nine hours of their absence for I feared
lest the Mists should come on, and so keep them on
the heights all night, but not a Cloud came to distress
them and not one of the party were any worse for the
expedition. On the following week we had illuminations,
Trans[formations?] and a balloon at Ld. S.'s on the other
side the Lake, with elegant refreshments, & a great deal of
good company—we took all the older children & on these
occasions his Ldship always sends his caraige to fetch &
carry us home.

I heard of you my dear Sir, some time ago, from M^r
Rickman who mentioned your having become executor
to a wealthy man of the name of Kick [?], with many interesting circumstances connected therewith—also, I understood you were in a commission of Defence, the duties
of which important office you will no doubt perform
better than our good friend & neighbour Mr Calvert,
who tells us there is no redress for having the windows

beaten in at midnight, *frame & all*, if the rogues do not *enter & rob*—nor for wringing the necks of chickens, and leaving them half dead tied by the heels to a tree. Do you know any thing at present of Mr Kenyon? I was exceedingly affected by a most uncommon mark of liberality & benevolence in that gentleman; he made a proposal to Mr Southey to assist Hartley with a small sum during his residence at College, he was told that H. with strict economy might make his allowance do, he then begged that he might pay 20£ per annum for the next five years, for the benefit of Mr C's other son whose education might be forwarded better by this addition, it was accepted, & he sent the first payment immediately; *this for yourself alone.*

Gen. & Mrs Peachey dined with C. at Mr Bowles's near Calne, the Marquis of Lansdown was there and several others & C. was very eloquent: also, they heard him speak for 3 quarters of an hour at the "Bible Society" at Calne, & they saw him & H. at the play-performance [of] the "Remorse", well enacted. H. is a most ardent admirer of Shakespere, which pleases Sir George, and his admiration of W's "Excursion" delights her Ladyship, who almost worships this Poet—she would not exchange the pleasure she derives from his Poems, for any earthly consideration. You will be pleased to hear that D. was told by 2 fellow Collegians of his brother, that he had read hard during the term, that his Greek was commended by the Warden, & that he received 2 Classical books as presents for good conduct—pray that this may last. Yesterday a Gentleman, fellow of —— College Oxford drank tea here; he spoke as knowing Mr Ward [and] of having been at Stowey; Mr J. Ward was also his acquaintance; he told me a great deal of Bristol, his name is Simmons. Another & another year rolls on, & we do not see you, & now I fear there is less likelihood than ever; I should like to see you once more I confess, if I should ever go to Bristol, would you permit me to go to see you at Stowey? You would be pleased with my little Sara, she is thought an interesting little creature, & I assure [you], very amiable; how can her father bear to absent himself so long from her, I am sure he loves her notwithstanding. But I hear wonders of your dear Niece beside those you tell me; she was 17 I think in May; I dare say she is much taller than Hartley; he has not grown for the last year or two; I think his father must have been surprized to see him so little grown: Derwent and Sara begin to grow rather faster than [they] did at any former period; but the latter is so delicate that I [dare] not let her study much; indeed she has always had her full share of play, & certainly more pleasure than falls to the lot of children in general; for Southey chuses to take the children on the water whenever a party is going from the house and as this generally lasts all day, and occurs pretty often they certainly have too much of this sort of thing during the summer; & Sara is almost half her time at Greta-bank with Miss Calvert where she rides on horseback often and plays more than half her time: I trouble you with these trifles, to shew you that she is not made ill by books; for I have not the slightest doubt if anything ill should happen to this dear child there would not be wanting persons to say, that she had been kept too close [at her studies.] I am half ashamed of sending this long and troublesome epistle, after threatening you with a few lines only; I could go on as far again if it were not for shame, and that my paper is ended. God bless you dear Mr Poole—remember me kindly to Mr King when you see him & believe me ever, with regards your truly affec. friend   S. C.

Please to give my best regards to Mr Ward & if any of my late Stowey friends enquire for me say, I think of them often & should rejoice to see them again.

12

[April, 1816]

My dear Sir

Can you tell me where Mr Kenyon is now? If you have not yet seen the account in the newspapers, you will be shocked & grieved to hear from me, that Southey has just followed to the Grave his only Son, Herbert, who departed this life on Wednesday last, in the tenth year of his age, after an illness of six weeks; and never was child more lamented by a father than this is, and will be to the latest hour of his life.

The body was opened on Thursday, & the disease was discovered to be seated in the heart—wherein was found a very large quantity of matter—nearly a quart—part of which was quite pure, the rest mingled with blood—it seems, no human skill could have arrested the disease, & this is a satisfaction to the parents, who were continually lamenting the distance from London & Edinburgh,

& sometimes talked of sending for Dr Southey from Town: Southey thinks he never shall be the happy Man he has been & I greatly fear it too: My poor Sister is not to be consoled, at present—the Almighty will, I trust, enable them to bear their affliction, & time will, no doubt, do something for them! but they are deeply smitten, & sorely wounded by this dreadful visitation! They have four Daughters left, the youngest three years old; I do not expect they will have any more children, but *yet*, it *may* be so.

You will be much affected, as will all who know Southey, on reading the Proem of the "Poet's Pilgrimage", the last proof sheet of which has just been put into his hands, from the post—"Oh," he exclaimed, "what a difference between the first proof sheet, and the last!" The poem opens with his "Return" wherein he speaks of his whole family, mentioning that dear boy, in a very peculiar manner, and the poor child was so delighted at what was said about him, and leaped around the study, repeating some of the lines rejoicing his fond father's heart —but I will write no more on this distressing subject.

Mr Coleridge is gone to London to present his Play, which he calls, a "Christmas Tale", or two Plays in one, something in the way of the "Winter's Tale",—it includes a Prelude & 4 acts; he says in his letter to me, a few weeks before he left Calne "My reason, or rather necessity, for giving my Xmas Tale, to Covent-Garden, is this, that two thirds of its success will depend on the manner in which three female characters are acted, *all* prominent, though not equally so, and each altogether distinct from the other

43

two. Now there is not a single actress at Drury-Lane.
Poetical passages I have as carefully avoided, as in the
'Remorse' I sought them." Are you not surprized at my
receiving a letter? The first for almost three years! and
the delay caused by no possible reason; none even assigned. I do not know his Town address, but I have written to Lamb & hope he will soon send it me, and some
account of his success, or otherwise. I rather suspect that
the Play is not accepted or I think he would have written,
if all had been well.—Hartley came home at the Xmas
vacation, & though we were all rejoiced to see him, yet we
regretted much the necessity of his coming so many miles,
on the outside of the Coach at that bitter season of the
year—next Christmas, he must, I think, spend at Ottery,
as each of his Uncles has sent him a kind invitation to go
thither, either at the next long vacation or when it best
suits him to go—but I think he must come home in June—
as his friends the Beaumonts, wish much to see him, and
intend bringing young G. Beaumont (Sir G. B.s cousin, &
heir) who is about 17—an Eton Boy, to see the country,
and Ly B. says—"I think Mrs Coleridge, he & Hartley
will suit each other, although George is no genius; at any
rate he may read Greek with H. & talk of Mathematics
and play with Derwent—and he will tell them something
of their cousins—the Coleridges, who, I understand are
two of the cleverest Boys at Eton School."

Hartley tells me that his cousin John, of the Temple,
has been at Oxford taking his Master's degree; he likes
him much, and was treated by him in the most friendly
manner; all this is well; & all will, I hope, continue so if

poor H: is but careful in the management of his affairs, which will require his very best attention & I really believe he has no one expensive habit at present. I could not per[suade] him to go back in the inside of the Coach, on account of the expence, although the weather was so . .? . . his return at Christmas.—You were so kind as to ask about Derwent, who is much [improved]; he is head Boy at Mr Danes' School in both the Greek & Latin Classes; he perseveres in his mathematical Studies, & I understand has made a good progress. He was fortunate enough last Summer to get some instruction from a Mr Nihil, a student of St John's Cambridge—who says he is a very clever Lad, and for his age, and the time he has learnt, an uncommonly good mathematician; he left him several books on leaving Ambleside & wrote him a very handsome letter wherein he tells him that if he can get to Cambridge in a couple of years time he has no doubt of his being able to distinguish himself soon—since this, the poor fellow dreams of nothing else; and is sanguine enough to hope that something will turn up for him by the time he is old enough to go—"in the meantime, Mother", he says, "I will work hard, I will leave nothing undone that can be accomplished by labour, & I have free permission to visit Mr Lockhart, (a great Mathematician in the neighbourhood of the School,) and to tell him of any new thing that I have done".

Sara & Edith are at Rydal-Mount, they went off with one of the Wordsworths on the morning of our loss: Sara had a dangerous attack of Croupe a few weeks since: she is delighted at the hope of one of these days seeing you again, and of visiting her father's relations at Ottery, one of whom has written me a kind letter, and sent a very affectionate message to the dear little Girl. The account you gave of Mr Ward's happiness was very agreeable to me; I beg to be particularly remembered to him, he is a person for whom I always had a very great esteem.—I shall rejoice to see him—next to you, more than any other of my old friends; tell him, I do not forget his fondness for little Sara, Dear child! never did little orphan experience more general favour than she has ever done! every one has a caress ready for her; she has never yet known what unkindness is.

Wordsworth & his family are well & prosperous; his daughter went from hence after a long visit at Miss Barker's, with the 2 Girls: she is just 12 years old, & a fine sprightly Girl—his eldest Son is not given to books, he has great expectation from his youngest—a child of 5 years.—Poor Lloyd is in a private mad-house at York, from which he escaped a few weeks since, and came to this country—it is advised to send him to Dr Willis: his excellent wife is gone with her 4 daughters to live at Birm. her 4 Sons are left with Mr Dawes, to finish their education.   *   *   *

13

Greta hall, Saturday May 24*th* 1816

My dear Sir

Your letter was brought me last night at Greta-bank (Mr Calvert's) too late to thank you for it by return of Post; I hope you will not be made uneasy by the delay.—We are all much obliged by the solicitous enquiries you make for us; my poor brother & sister are deep mourners still, & will be, in some degree, I fear, to the end of life! Southey has, however, done great things, even in the bitterest days of his most bitter sorrow—he never did so much in the same space of time: he has begun & finished his Poem on the marriage of the *Princess*— it is called The "Lay of the Laureate"—I read the proof sheets as they were corrected, & much delighted I was with it, as well as surprized at seeing *such* a production at such a season produced; he is a most extraordinary being —good & great & deserves to be happy. Mr Richard Wordsworth, W's elder brother, is just dead: he died at Lambeth at his brother Christopher's house, who has just been presented to two valuable livings by his grace the Arch-B. of C. for which he has resigned the deanery of Bocking. R. W. had married, 18 months since, his servant maid, who kept his country house near Penrith—he has left an infant Son who will of course, with his Mother inherit the whole of his property. If this marriage had not taken place our friend would have had the Stockbridge estate, the maternal [?] inheritance, which, as his brother lived single to almost 50 years of age, he has always had great expectation of either for himself or his Son. Wordsworth is however well off in point of income—but will not have much to leave his 3 children at his death.

You will be sorry to hear the bad account I send you of poor S. T. C. He went to Town with his Play—it would not do, was returned for alteration, which instead of instantly setting about he got in a fit of despondency and was confined 3 weeks to his bed, where his friend Mr Morgan was obliged to attend him: they are now both in Town, and M. tells me he is fast recovering under a Physician at Highgate who undertakes to cure him of Opium: he will alter his play for next season.

You will also be sorry for another thing respecting him—Oh! when will he ever give his friends anything but pain? he has been so unwise as to publish his fragments of "Christabel" & "Koula-Khan" Murray is the publisher, & the price is 4s 6d—we were all sadly vexed when we read the advertizement of these things.

I am always much gratified by the accounts you send me of your interesting relation, Miss E. Poole, it gives me a very sensible pleasure to find that she is always in the enjoyment of the best state of health, notwithstanding her indefatigable attention to her studies: I sincerely pray that she may remain a comfort to you, to the end of your days!

Southey has just received a letter from Mr Kenyon, from the Lake of Geneva. We do not expect the Beaumonts here till the beginning of July: young Beaumont is not Sir G. B.s son, he is no nearer than second cousin, but he is his heir. Lloyd is still in confinement at York: they talk of removing him to Dr Willis: M^{rs} Ll. is coming again into the neighbourhood of Ambleside; she wishes to be with her sons during the Midsummer vacation, and it is easier for her to bring her daughters to them than to send for them to Birmingham.

—Hartley will be greatly pleased by your kind wish to

see him at dear Stowey when I shew him your letter;—he
will no doubt avail himself of it the first opportunity. I
think, though, if it were the same thing to you, that it
will be better for him to visit his western friends in the
summer vacation than at Xmas and spend the short Xmas
vacation nearer Oxford: he will probably be at .. [?] .. or
Bristol during that vacation which lasts only 5 weeks, &
the long summer vacation is full 4 months, during which,
he may, if nothing happen to prevent, pass a few weeks
with you and the remainder with his three uncles at
Ottery, all of whom have sent him an invitation to their
houses;—but I do not like to form plans for so great a
distance of time—heaven only knows if all, or any of us
may be in a condition to realize them—three months ago,
that precious little boy was rejoicing at his father's promises of taking him into the South—but I will not begin
upon this subject—would to God, we could lose sight of
it a little while, for indeed this is a most gloomy abode at
present, and the frequent-recurring tears of the unhappy
Mother distress even the very *least* of the Children and
make her often shed her own for very sympathy.—I had
a pleasant account of Sara on her return from her visit
at Rydal-Mount—Wordsworth had been so good as to
hear her read *Latin* and *Italian* daily, being, as I was told
by his sister, much pleased with her progress in the first
of these, & quite astonished at her knowledge of the last;
saying, she was a credit to herself & to her teacher. I am
however, my dear Sir, quite of your opinion respecting
these things, that the less is said about them the better—
and with regard to dear Sara, though she is thought much

of in these parts, because it so happens that she is a little beforehand with some of her young neighbours, yet you, who have been accustomed to one so very extraordinary, laugh at what others pretend to be astonished at—but the truth is that this child cannot be permitted to study as many hours in a day, as other children, on account of the delicacy of her constitution; she is, however, thank God, getting quite strong and growing very fast, she and Edith Southey are the same height—she is 14 months the elder of the two.

*　　*　　*

14

Greta hall, Keswick, June [1817]

My dear Sir

I ought, long since, to have sent you my best thanks for your kind reception of, & numerous friendly attentions to my Son Hartley on his visit to you last Summer: his letters from your pleasant dwelling were indicative of the most affectionate gratitude towards yourself and all around you for the revival of so many pleasing associations connected with the days of early childhood; & before I quit this, to me, affecting subject, I must also mention his *very particular sense* of Mrs R. Poole's manner towards him, which he said, "was uniformly Kind, & sometimes, I could almost fancy *even affectionate*". Of Miss P. he spoke in terms of unqualified admiration. Next to these he speaks, I think, of the Wards, and their delightful children; Mr W. (I am most happy to believe it) seems to have drawn a prize in the matrimonial lottery: present to him & his lady my sincere wishes for the continuance of their happiness.

You may not have heard of the present circumstances of my poor Derwent who left School last Sep^t in the hope that something would turn out to enable him to go to Cambridge; nothing immediately presented itself in the way of an Exhibition, (which if we get the promise of, we are not sure that [it] would be prudent to send him) or Scholarship, & he, not knowing exactly how to handle the course of his Studies, accepted an invitation to visit a Gentleman in Lancashire whose sons had been partly educated by his master Mr Dawes, but were then, at one of the great public Schools: during this visit he often saw a Gentleman of the name of Hopwood who paid him some attentions, asked him to his house &c—this, in short, ended in Derwent's consenting, by the advice of Mr Dawes, to live for a couple of years with Mr Hopwood as private Tutor to his two little boys preparatory to his sending them to Eton.—Never was astonishment greater than mine, when Mr Dawes wrote, saying that D. had been offered the situation, was willing to try it, and only waited for his uncle's, Mr Wordsworth's, & my advice on the subject. When I considered that he was but just turned of 17, & looked only 15 I was much afraid that he would not be able to [assume] sufficient authority for the situation; this objection was over-ruled, and on condition that he was to be at liberty if anything likely to settle him for life should occur, he made a final engagement. He is now at home to meet his brother whom we daily expect from Oxford, and on being asked how he likes his present way of life, he says, nothing on earth could induce him to pass a great many years of his life as a private Tutor; but he is determined to do his duty in it as long as he is in it; and the greatest difficulty he finds is, making the children tractable, which he says he could much easier do, if he was *older*, & *Mama* were not so *very* indulgent.— These boys are so indulged that the engagement was that they were only to be in the School-room 3½ hours, at 3 different times of the day, so that D. never sees them after 3 o'clock in the afternoon, when he takes his walks and comes home just in time for dinner at half past 5. At half past 6 he is again at Liberty and reads in his own appartment till 9 when he goes to tea, & the rest of the evening is his own, either to stay in the Drawing room, or in his own room; so you see he is not overworked; but he says, if they were not uncommonly quick, he could do but little for them in so short an allotment of time. His salary is 50 guineas per annum.—Sometime last year S. T. C. wrote to tell us, that Mr Freere had promised to try to get a Tutored-Scholarship for D. and the poor lad was in extacies in the hope of this; but we have heard nothing of it since. I should like much to get him into one of the public offices, if it were possible, but he thinks he has not health for constant writing in an office; & I tell him, his health would be much more tried by studying Mathematics at Cambridge.—I was in some hope, my dear Sir, of being able to tell you that H. had gained the prize for English-verse this year, and delayed my letter of thanks to you *in* that hope, which has proved falacious, as that honour was adjudged to Mr Ormrod of New-College: H's letter announcing his failure was written in a half witty, half phylosophic style, which amused us much.

Mr Kenyon is at Aix-la-Chapelle. Southey has written to him there in answer to a very kind one addressed to me: his wife is not in good health; he is going to Spa.—Do you remember about 21 years ago, a Physician, Dr May, on a visit at Roskilly's?, I think he drank tea once at our cottage and gave me some advice about weaning Hartley, &c. &c. This man wrote a note to Southey, saying, he should do himself the honour of calling on him, that he was an old acquaintance of Mrs Coleridge's and well known to Dr Southey being a member of the same College. S. invited him to breakfast next day, and we were amused by his account of a ten years' captivity in france; and he took leave saying he was that day to dine with Sir Frederick Moorshead, and meant to call immediately on Mr Edmond . . ? . . our good Apothecary, saying, we medical Men need no introduction to each other. S. had a bad cold, and did not return his visit at his Lodgings, and, we have now great reason to rejoice at this, for during the few weeks he has lived in this town, he has played a number of most odd pranks, amongst others, calling upon sick people, telling them they would die if they did not take his prescriptions, and in one instance making the Son of a poor dissenting minister give him 5 guineas for a forced visit to his Mother (for whom he did not prescribe as she was dying at the time;) he having previously told Mr E. that even if he were called in, he never charged anything to the dissenting Clergy as they were so ill paid; in

consequence of this, and some other shabby pieces of
petty roguery he was soon sent to Coventry, and yesterday
the Gentleman took a french leave, in debt to 8 or 10
persons—some 40, some 50 shillings, and in one instance
in the neighbourhood of Low-Wood, as much as £20!
Some of the Tradespeople went after him, but he could
not satisfy the full demand of any of them. So much for
Dr May!—

My dear Sir, I have kept this letter a long time as M^r
Rickman had intended us a visit and might have franked
it, and in the hope of hearing first from you, as I have now
done from your letter by Mrs Skurray, for I was not sure
but you might be abroad: we are most glad to hear good
news of you, but if your letter had announced a visit to us,
it would have been still more welcome. Wordsworth has
just left the room (with Mrs S. who is a great favorite here)
and in going out he said—"For God's sake, do ask Poole
why he does not come to see us."—I replied I have asked
him so often, I fear he will think it a persecution, & I feel
assured he will come as soon as it is in his power. I will
look forward to next year with some *hope* at least.—
Hartley has been at home some time & is working hard
for his examination, but we have so much interruption
from perpetual company during his vacation, that he
sometimes thinks of carrying off his books to some quiet
nook in Borrowdale, for the remaining weeks of the vacation; Sir G. B., who is now here always, considerately
says remember we expect Hartley whenever Mrs S. comes
to us, & whenever else he feels inclined, but do not let him
be *urged* to come, if he had rather stay with his books;

54

he will go to-day to meet Mr Skurray at Mr Calverts, and
after *that* no more dinners,—Hartley spent a most pleasant week with Mrs King at Bristol; for her attentions to
him I am also greatly Obliged: every body is good and
kind to my dear children, & for this, when I am inclined
to murmur at my misfortunes I reserve a feeling of thankfulness & gratitude.—Gen: Peachey & his Lady were at
Oxford during the Commemoration (he is a Doctor of
civil Laws)—when he understood that H. had written *for*,
and *not* gained the prize, he, in a very handsome manner,
enclosed for him a Sum nearly approaching to that which
he would have gained by the prize, thereby evincing his
good opinion of the talents of the unsuccessful candidate.
You will, I doubt not join with me and his other anxious
friends in wishing him better success in his application
for a fellowship which he will try for after he has taken
his degree in the Spring & if he fail, poor fellow! he must
be content to take orders with no better view than a
curacy, which has been the fate of many a wiser & better
than he, God bless him.

—Southey is printing his *Life of John Westley*, & third
Vol: of Brasil; he is writing a letter to Mr Brou[gh]am,
and he has various other works on hand, but I believe he
has not attempted Poetry since the death of the dear
child; but he is cheerful, & strangers think him the happiest Man alive: but my sister betrays her increasing regret daily & hourly, & at this time her spirits are more
than ordinarily bad, although she occasionally has
laughed at Mr Skurray's west-country anecdotes which
have greatly amused us all & none more than the two

elder Girls, who are just at an age to relish such entertainment. They had no idea of the Somersetshire provincial dialect till they heard him give us it in perfection, but they will not allow that it is *half* as pleasing as the Cumberland, which they assume at pleasure & are much amused at the blunders I make when I attempt the genuine Cumberland tongue. By the bye, I enjoy exceedingly hearing H or D. read the popular scottish Novels, they give the true scottish accent to those particular parts, giving them much effect, according to my judgement.—I have had frequent letters, and some remittance from my husband during the last year; H. passed both the Christmas & Easter vacations with him at Mr Gilman's. M^r & Mrs Wordsworth saw him in the winter; he is *quite grey haired*; he was much agitated at seeing them, but was very agreeable on the whole. Mrs G. Coleridge tells me, that his brother, the Colonel, was much pleased with his society in Town in the Spring, and a gentleman a friend of Col. C.'s thought he had never been so agreeably entertained in his life; and that S. T. C. was the most astonishingly eloquent Man he had ever seen.—These accounts of his long-absent parent, make my dear, affectionate boy, Derwent most eager to see his father, & I think, whatever is the consequence he *shall* go up to Town at the next summer vacation, for there is [no] chance of seeing him here, & for myself I have long ceased to wish it.

May I request the favour, dear Mr Poole, of some little account of the Brice's & Cruckshanks's next time you are so good as to send me a few lines: tell also, of Miss Seager.—I had a most kind letter from my friend Miss

Chorter a few months since, I was in hope of seeing her &
her sister at the Island this year, but they cannot bear the
thought of it: I have promised to spend a little time with
them at Taunton whenever I visit the West of England.
Two Gentlemen of Oxford, who dine here to-morrow,
brought letters from John Coleridge; they bring the news
of his Marriage, and that he is gone with his Bride to
Ottery.

—Southey begs to be most kindly remembered to
you, and joins Wordsworth & myself in ardent wishes to
see you in the North. Hartley sends his kindest regards
to yourself & all his agreeable Stowey friends; and love
to the sweet little Wards.—And now it is quite time to
release you; for you have a very ill-written scrawl to
Wade through which I really ought to apologize for, having spun out to such a length.

God bless you. Believe your truly affectionate & obliged
friend

S. C.

I forgot to tell you that Mr Lloyd & his eldest son have
been staying with us for some little time past; Ll. is not
cured by his residence with Dr Willis, but he is quite sane
in company so that you would not know that all is not
right unless alone; poor fellow, I have the greatest pity
for him. Hartley called on him at Birm: on his way home,
Ll. was so rejoiced at seeing him that he would not leave
him out of his sight. He staid a fortnight, and he wanted
to make him engage to do the like on his return, but H.
will not have time. His Son is a fine youth of 18, as tall

as his father. He has 8 children, & his aimable wife is a prey to the greatest anxiety on his account, God comfort her, poor Soul! her sorrows are *far* beyond mine.

I should not have troubled you with a double letter, if S. had not offered to send this to his friend for a frank.

15

Netherhall July 21st 1817

My dear Sir

Your kind letter was a confirmation of most welcome tidings to me, & was indeed, doubly welcome, as it convinced me that you still take a lively interest in our concerns, a circumstance able to afford me a higher pleasure than I can now express, having only time, from the lateness of the hour, and my extreme weariness, to thank [you] for it most heartily, & to threaten you with a very long epistle at S.'s return, full of family matters, adventures of the Lake Poets—&c &c for which I intend to obtain a frank.

I must, however, just inform you that S. has met Mr Kenyon at H. W. Williams's, at Paris & afterwards dined with him & his Lady at their own house; this interview was unexpected, and very pleasant to all parties.

My sister Southey & myself are here with our two Girls; Edith has been ill; she & her cousin bathe in the Sea [which] has been useful to both; but Sara, thank

God! is in very good health, & has been so for nearly a year past.

Mr Senhouse, the owner of this pleasant dwelling is abroad with Southey: both his family are here & we are as happy as we can be deprived of his society; Mr Senhouse is a very pleasant & a very accomplished Man; Southey thought himself fortunate in his proposal to accompany him to France, Italy &c &c.

Derwent is at School at present; he had the pleasure of a visit of 6 weeks here in the Spring—his Master, Mr Dawes, when he had been here a week, on being applied to, said, he should grant a longer stay with very particular pleasure; for he thought he had confined himself far too much during the last winter—he is of opinion that *all* study, & *no* play is not good for boys; and he concluded his permission with saying, that he should appear very unlike a School-master, he feared, in what he had said about relaxation but he had, at that time, no other pupil, who gave occasion to him to give similar advice to him. The truth is, that my poor D. has been trying hard to fit himself for Cambridge, in the hope that Dr Saterthwaite Chaplain to Ld Lonsdale, might succeed in getting an exhibition for him: this having failed, he must direct his thoughts, his hopes, and calculations into a different channel; and endeavour to reconcile himself to other scenes, than "Academic Bowers": but Mr Dawes says, "if he were my son, & I could afford it, I certainly should send him to Cam."—There is one thing that reconciles me to the poor Lad's disappointment—i.e.—that I really think his ambition to take a high degree would be the means of injury to his health, for he is not among the strongest:—more on this subject anon.

H. has written twice for the "english poetical prize", but failed each time; his verses, however, are not bad, & his Uncle, between ourselves, has no doubt but his last year's was as good as the prize—the youth himself says it was *not*, & that he should have had no hesitation in deciding for M'Donald—H. is always upon honour, & in points like these, has no self-love to mislead him; but alas, poor youth never was a more excentric creature ever walked the earth. I must say adieu! There are 24 persons in the drawing room at Tea, & Sara tells me they are wondering where Mrs Coleridge is—we are just returned from an al fresco dinner 2 miles up the valley, by a brook side, and I am so tired that I can scarcely see for weariness—to say the truth, I am grown too old for these things, and have no pleasure in them but what I derive from seeing the enjoyment of the young persons of the party.

Mrs Lovell's Son is with her at Keswick, come to pass the summer with her after an absence of 7 years, think what a scene the meeting was!—and the poor youth was no doubt much mortified at his Mother's astonishment at his appearance, which was shabby in the extreme; he having by his own choice, walked all the way from town 300 miles and having been wetted successively through & through for the last 3 days:—Robert is a very shrewd youth, and not being endowed with any of those overweening sensibilities which, I am sorry to say, distinguish his 2 cousins H & D., I think he is much more likely to be happy & perhaps to confer happiness, or, I should rather say more likely to escape giving pain to others than those whose minds and manners are so intirely different from his.

If you had met C. a few days later—that is, on the 19th or 20th of the month—Hartley would have had the happiness of seeing you, for he left Oxford on the 18th to join his father at Highgate—God bless you, my dear friend; I hope this short scrawl will find you safe at dear Stowey; that place with which I have so many associations: but I must not begin upon that subject—How it thunders this longest day of the year!—

So then, the state prisoners are acquitted!—

Sara's best regards and Mrs S's unite with mine, who am my dear, dear Mr P. yours with affection & respect.

S. COLERIDGE

Do remember me in the Kindest manner to my friend Mr Ward; tell him I long to see his dear little ones, and that I never will forget his kindness to mine; tell him, that if ever my Sara has the happiness to see him again, that I expect him to like her as well as he certainly did in the year 1807.

There is no getting pens, ink & paper even at Netherhall where all good things abound, as completely as one can at one's own house.—I was obliged to [send] the butler for these and they are wretched.

16

Greta hall, *Keswick*, *Sunday*. *Sept*. 1818

Dear friend,

I am indeed, very proud to find my poor letters have the power to interest you—nay, it is *not* pride, it is a feeling that brings a consolation with it; & the continuance of your friendship through so many long & to me, anxious years, shall be classed among the many blessings I am permitted to enjoy. Your kind solicitude about us induces me to give you a little sketch of the history of this day, *this little day*, which, although not marked by anything that may be deemed a misfortune, has nevertheless, been made up of vexatious incidents, mingled with a few others of a different character.—At the hour of nine we all assembled at the breakfast table— S. his wife & two eldest daughters, myself & Sara, all well, except the good Lady of the house, who is in a very complaining way at present, (Mrs Lovell always breakfasts *alone* in the School-room & Hartley *alone* in his Study). A note is brought in—S^ir G. & Ly. B's compliments hope to see the whole party to dinner including the young Ladies. We promise to go—

Away fly the 2 cousins to Shake the Pear-tree before dressing for Church—in a minute, Edith enters, breathless—"Aunt Coleridge, Sara has shaken something out of the Tree, into her Eye, & she is distracted with the pain". After bathing the Eye & lamenting over it, & deprecating the *folly* of the poor sufferer for near an hour, S. raps at the

62

door with all the children ready for church, except one. Where is Kate? "She has such a bad head-ach she cant go to Church, her Mother is going to stay with her to give her James's-Powder, so I hope Sara is better & you are both ready for church." Sara was too blind to go, but I huddled on my things and got to Church as the last Psalm was reading, found our pew full, obliged to go into another, & when the communion plate was brought round, had left my purse at home, & sitting among Strangers looked very foolish. When Church was over, "Where's Miss Coleridge?" from the Beaumonts, Peacheys, Calverts,—all prescribed a different remedy for the inflamed organ, & the kind B's hoped she would be well enough before 4 o'clock to meet them at dinner, & that Kate would not keep her Mama at home. On our return, Kate was in a high fever; Mama very unhappy, poor Aunt Lovell on the Couch in her *very worst way*, & on entering the bedroom, I found it quite darkened, and Sara in tears. "Now Mama, say not one word about my going with you, but let me lie quietly on this bed & you shall find me here on your return at night." At ½ past 3, the patients being no better, Southey with his eldest daughter set off, bearing the apologies of all the rest, Hartley had before excused himself, that he might have a long, quiet day to read. We sent off for the D^r who tried with a camel's-hair pencil to clear the lid of the eye, but made it worse; prescribed for Kate, who was put to bed, and Sara lay down again in despair, & I sat by her bed-side reading . . ? . . Bible till 5 o'clock when your welcome letter was brought which giving a sort of fillip to the patient, she rose, & begged me to go down with her to Tea, to the party, which with sister Edith's persuasion I accordingly did. No sooner were we seated at the Tea-table Mr Collins, Artist, turns to me & says; "Have you read Blackwood['s] last number, (Magazine)?" No,—I understand Mr Wm Hazlitt is about to commence a prosecution against the Editor of that work, for a libel, & Mr Hartley Coleridge is the Author of the same; this is the report at Edinburgh from whence I arrived last night.

We all laughed at the idea of accusing Hartley of this piece of personality who would be the last person to write such an article, as he disapproves of anything of the sort; but I was annoyed at hearing of the intended prosecution, because Southey & Wordsworth may be troubled to give their evidence to the truth of the assertions in the article which would be very disagreeable, & as Master Hazlitt will cut a very ridiculous figure, I wonder he chuses to make a stir in it. I think I told you the ridiculous story of Hazlitt's behaviour to a Peasant Girl when he was here 12 or 14 years ago: some person has taken up this tale, mentioning the kindness of Mr Wordsworth and others to him on this occasion, & commenting on his ingrati-tude: W. spoke of it here last week & seemed vexed that his name was connected with the thing in any way; but so it is.—Well, the eye grew more troublesome, & I pro-posed returning home; Sir George seemed so much con-cerned, that he seconded me, saying he thought S. would be easier in bed.—Just as she had got into bed, & I had hardly prepared myself to be with her for the night, (fearing to disturb her, by going at a later hour) the maid comes up—Ma'am, here are two Gentlemen who *must* see you, they are friends of Mr Coleridge:—"pray call Hartley to them, I am nearly undressed," "Mr Hartley is just gone to the Inn with Mr Lloyd's servant, who says, his Master is very wild & uneasy to-night, and begs him to sit beside him for awhile"—"dear me" Well, after sitting a full hour with these Gents: I suffered them to depart without asking them to stay supper, for which I got a trimming from S. who did not venture to ask them himself not being *sure* whether there was anything in the house to give them, as he had dined out.—It is now 12 o'clock & as poor Sara was sweetly sleeping, instead of going to bed, I have sat scribbling to you these *important* adventures, which I hardly dare send off lest you should say, "Phaw. What nonsense." All this might do very well from Mrs C. to one of her Sisters but what care I? I am determined however the Rigmarole shall cost nothing & now good night. Tuesday evening.—Your second letter came at the usual hour of five, at the dinner Table; but having company I could not finish my letter in time to send it to Mr Rickman to-night: I hope you will not be uneasy at the delay. Poor Sara's Eye is much enflamed still about the Lid, but the cause is removed by Sleep; little Katherine is not quite well yet.—Our party this evening was Mr Dauncey, counsellor, his two Daughters, & a Miss MacTaggart, with 3 Oxford Youths, & Miss Christian, sister to Mr Curwan member for this County; & tomorrow we have the whole party from the Island to dinner, 6 in number, and Southey expects a Young

Gentleman in the morning to stay here till the Cambridge term commences; he is a most interesting young Man, who, having written to Southey three years since has become a regular correspondent: S. has only seen him for one half hour, but we have all seen his letters & his poetry, and are all full of curiosity for a sight of him except Hartley, who cannot afford the time to pay him any attention which as he is a very young Man, only 20, I am sorry for, as it would relieve his Uncle sometimes.

This Mr Chancey Hare Townshend is the only Child of very rich parents who have a great fear that he will become a Poet, & wish to associate with none but Men of letters, on which account they have never until now permitted him to come to Southey; nor would his father for a long time let him go to the University; so I guess there is no great sympathy between them. I remember an expression in his first letter. "I am a spoilt child of Affluence with no human being within my reach to whom I can communicate my thoughts & feelings." If my dear Derwent were here they would be excellent companions, if I have judged rightly of Mr Townshend, for he is full as romantic, & abstracted as ever his poor father was at his age, & I should imagine this youth to be somewhat in the same way. S. tells us he is quite an Adonis!

Before I take my leave I must not forget to tell you, that I rather think the Letter to Brougham is given up; & if so, I shall be rather glad than sorry, for it was a *tartar*.

The Kenyons are to pass the winter in Italy: I remember Mr Best, a very clever, well informed person; not so his inane partner, if I have a right Idea of Mrs B. I am

sorry for Miss Brice's illness; &, I was going to say, for
the embarrasments of the Cruckshanks's, but I am *not*
quite so sure of that; and I should be afraid of some mis-
managements in that quarter; yet I do wish them well for
all that. Mr Skurry was indeed very popular among us;
but may I venture to confess that I thought more highly
of his understanding in the Pulpit than I did in a room;
notwithstanding his entertaining powers: the Beaumonts
were of the same mind; they both think well of Hartley
as a Theologian, & speak with much partial commendation of him at all times: he is to be with them at Coleorton
after he has taken his degree. My dear friend, you pass
over in silence my request respecting H.'s *habits*, &
manners as a visitor in your hospitable dwelling; I wished
to know, as he is a little apt to procrastinate at home,
whether he was more on his guard abroad or not: I shall
be in a great fright about him when he is at Coleorton-
hall lest he should sometimes be too late at Table: he is
most tormenting in that respect when he dares to take the
liberty of coming in after the time. When I quitted the
subject of Mr Skurry a little abruptly to speak of H. I did
not mean any comparison to the prejudice of Mr S. nor
dare I flatter myself that H. will acquit himself half as
well as that Gentleman seems to do in the department in
which he is destined to move; but it just then occurred
to me what the Beaumonts had said, at the same time
when they spoke of Mr S., & I thought you would be
pleased to hear it. Mr Collins, who is on a visit to Sir
George, has made a likeness of Sara in an Oil painting,
in the character of Wordsworth's "Highland Girl":

Wordsworth admires the picture but objects to S's style of person & character of countenance, for that subject; she, he thought might do for a Sylph, or for many other subjects better than that *one*: however, the painter likes it, so does his patron so it is to be in the exhibition next Spring. Mr Collins is a great admirer of C. and means to show him this likeness of his daughter when he returns to Town; I fear poor Samuel will be made uncomfortable by seeing it, & then good Mr Collins will feel mortified, for he does not know him well enough to understand the extreme excentricity of his character.—Sara is reading Don Quixote in the original Spanish.—Some other of poor H's friends as well as dear Mr Poole thought his Poem of last year, might have gained the prize, but as Doctors differ it was not to be: he says, he quite hates the poem of *this* year, and will not repeat it to any of us; tis very odd he does not bring home a Copy of his performance— I have no doubt at all but you are sometimes attacked on the subject of the *Apostacy of the Bards*, so am I, I generally refer them to the parties themselves, when that is possible.

Mr Wilberforce & his family are to be in Keswick on friday for 8 or 10 days, I shall be most delighted to see that good man, but, we have had such a succession of company & visiting lately that I shall not be sorry when the quiet season is setled in; for I am not fond of seeing such a number of strangers, I like to see the "old familiar faces" better: I therefore wish you would bring hither your "old familiar face."—Wordsworth talks of sending his eldest Son to the Charter-house [and his] daughter is

SARA COLERIDGE

at a genteel boarding school in [the neigh]bourhood; his youngest Son goes by day to Mr Dawes, his sons are not good learners, & poor W. frets a little about it, John is a very amiable Boy; the Girl is sharp, but not very steady, as yet, she is 14.—Hartley leaves us next week, before the Term, for the sake of Books, the next two months will be an anxious time for *him*, his *brother* & *sister* & *mother*; I must endeavour to be thankful come what will, & I think verily he will not disgrace the name which now stands high at both Universities—

God bless you my dear Sir, believe me ever most truly yours, & thank you for y^r letter &c

S. C.

17

[April, 1819]

My dear friend

You will start at the sight of a folio sheet; but I have much to say, and some news to impart which I^m sure will give you pleasure. To begin with the most recent, and consequently nearest my heart, i.e. Hartley Coleridge has had the singular good-fortune to be elected Fellow of Oriel-College, Oxford! I can hardly believe it possible; for I expected he would be obliged to make many trials for a fellowship before he would obtain one; to be elected *at once*, and *at Oriel*, is so truly desirable for him that all our friends are more than I can express, satisfied with the event.—I wrote a note to my friends at Rydal-mount (by Coach) as soon as the news arrived,

and in answer, my kind friend Dorothy, after saying all
for herself and family that her good heart dictated, further
says, "We rec^d the Oxford paper soon after your letter;
and an account from Mr Wm Jackson (Fellow of Queen's)
that H. C. had acquired great honour in his examination
for Oriel."—He told them that he was invited to dine with
the Fellows the next day; a distinction of which I daresay
he was not a little proud. H. had very little hope himself
that he should succeed, for his competitors were most of
them older than himself, and had been accustomed to
similar Trials, had had more regular classical training, i.e.
had been at the public Schools, (a great advantage we
now find in gaining classic honours) "and for all I know,"
said he "are my superiors in natural abilities". He, therefore, went to bed on Thursday night with a full determination to sleep out the *ringing of the Bells* which would peal
to the happiness of his rivals next day; when, sitting and
yawning over a late breakfast, the welcome annunciation
was brought in, which he thought must be only a deceitful
dream, so much was he stunned by the tidings, until the
succession of fees, with their "impenarative faces"
stamped the thing real.

Little William Wordsworth on his return in the evening
from School told his Mother, that he never saw *master* in
such a good humour in his life: "as soon as he got the
letter about Hartley, he rose up, gave a shout, and pro-
claimed a *holiday*": "the boys all huzza'd and there was
such an uproar, Mother!"

H. is now at the Isle of Wight with one of his pupils;
on his return he will have an important business to settle;

his removal from Merton; payment of debts; getting into Lodgings, [where] he *must* be for the next term to attend his Pupils, (some of whom are studying for their examination.) In July he may have the rooms assigned to him in ~~Merton~~ Oriel. (You see I wrote Robert for Richard in my confusion.) I think father was a little galled that the student did [not] reach the *first class*: but it must be considered, that he was a big boy when he began anything like regular scholarship:—he was only at a private school, never had any private Tutor (poor fellow, he fagged hard last long vacation, by himself, and refused to join any party of pleasure, even when Mr Townsend was here, scarcely ever dining out, except with the Beaumonts on sunday. Yet he said to me one day, "I'm *sure* I could get the thing done, if I could afford a good private tutor; but 50 guineas are *not to be had*, so poor *I* must take my chance"; "I suppose I shall come in second." This was, as you have heard, the truth)—so that all things considered no blame could reasonably fall on the lad, if he could not reach the rank which his cousins had reached before him, wanting their advantages; and Southey, Wordsworth and Sir George B. and many others said, he gained as much credit in his circumstances, being *second*, as some of those, who had hundreds bestowed on their education did in being *first*; however, all is now right.

In the next place my dear Sir, I have the pleasure to tell you that Southey has *another* son, a fine little fellow of two months old: my poor sister has suffered much on his account and still is suffering but I trust when these

easterly winds subside she will be able to leave her
chamber.—Southey is printing the 3ᵈ vol: of his "Brasil"
and the "Life of Westley" is in the press; he has numerous
things on hand but as soon as Edith is better he means to
shake the dust from his feet, and take flight towards the
Metropolis; he ought to go in a few weeks or he will be
absent at that time of the year when we see the more
interesting Lakers. The letter to Mʳ Brougham was given
up, and I rejoiced at it, for it would have provoked a
reply, and there would have [been] nothing but uneasiness
for us females who hate anything like a paper contest. S.
has two poems in hand, the one called "*Oliver Newman*",
the other "*the maid of Paraquay*": but they will not shew
their faces yet.

Yesterday we received our copies of Wordsworth's
"Peter Bell", it is a singular performance, the prologue is
very beautiful in its way: I daresay you will have read it
by this time, it was begun and partly written at the time
of W's residence in your parts.

You, perhaps, do not know that Wordsworth is, like
yourself, a *Justice of peace*: I spent the Christmas month
with him & his family, and many a laugh had we at him
about this same "*Justice*" which then he had not undertaken, and I think the ladies were much against it, thinking it would break in upon his poetic musings and that
he would not be able to perform the duties of it; but his
son John, a youth in his sixteenth year, a very good, sweet
tempered lad; but without one spark of imagination, [or] the
slightest feeling for the importance of his father's studies,
gave it, *as his opinion*, that his father would be employing

a part of his time *very wisely* in undertaking the office, for J. Carter, the Clerk, was able to do almost all belonging to the distribution of the taxes. Wordsworth has enough on his hands; for he is educating this youth, besides all his other occupations; as to letter-writing, *that* he has ever done by proxy.

I have had a few letters from C. lately who is in his *better way*. I am afraid his lectures were not very profitable to him, as he has not made me any remittance in consequence; Ly. B. wrote to say she had seen him in Grosvenor-Square, and he was in better spirits than she had hoped to find him. The picture which I named to you last year, as painted by Collins, of Sara, was given by the artist to her father, and it seems, he is delighted at the posse[ssion]

My second son Derwent is still at Summerhill, and in high . . ? . . but we are not without hope that we shall be able to send [him] next year to one of the universities; we have a prospect of part of the means for his support; and if fortune favour him as much as she has done his elder brother, he will obtain his heart's most ardent desire; but such good things as Merton-postmasterships are not to be had every day; yet our friends think that if he could get there, i.e. to College he might stand for a Scholarship, and obtain one: he will save a few pounds of his earnings for his fitting out.

I must now tell you a little secret tale which will not fail to interest you. Grosvenor C. Lloyd, eldest son of C. Lloyd, is the same age with Derwent, they were schoolfellows and affectionately attached to each other. He is in his grandfather's bank at Birm: and lives with him and his wife: he has, for pocket money, from 50 to 60 pounds per annum. One day, his mother, (worthy of such a son,) asked him to assist her in a sum of ten pounds which she was begging for a poor widow in distress; he said he would readily contribute: and now Mother I have a favour to beg in return; I am uneasy about Derwent for I think he is fit for nothing but a College life; he likes no profession *but* the Church: I wish you would not oppose my wish, if anything is [? agreed to] by his friends, of giving him all I can *so well spare* out of my money, and I can *with ease*, promise him at least £30 per annum towards his support at College, and I once heard Mr Wordsworth say he would help him a little, if the income-tax were taken off. His mother told him she thought it was an *excellent scheme*, and said she was soon going to Keswick, and would propose it to his mother and Uncle. "I shall tell D.," said this generous youth, "what I believe, that he would do as much for me, in the same circumstances, and that will persuade him to grant my request." Mrs Lloyd was here last Autumn, and told the thing; & when I spoke highly of Grosvenor for his sweet dispositions, she said; I don't see so much in it: Grosvenor wants for nothing, he will be provided for in the bank and I do not see how he can dispose of his money better. Poor Lloyd was with us last [summer]; he is in a wretched state of mind; it must be derangement. He is a most unhappy being and says he is *lost*, and that his wife & children are only shadows. I should fill a folio-sheet were I to tell you all his miserable fancies; he is an object [for] pity and his poor wife must have a wearisome time with him. I think I mentioned him in my last.

Sara is still very uneasy about not seeing her father. I hope I shall be able to take her to Town next year, when she may be gratified with a re-introduction to him, and then she must pay her long promised visit to Mrs Clarkson at Playford hall, and if possible, we shall extend on our journey to the west of England, for she longs to see the places inhabited by her parents in their youth; and those friends whose names she has so often heard mentioned with affection. Dear Mr Poole, I scarcely should have ventured this long, & egotistic epistle, if I could ever forget that he, whom I address, is the same person, who in days long past, made so many and such friendly exertions to render a miserable cottage, an abode of comparative comfort; the same, who some ten years since rec^d me and mine, under his hospitable roof with [? cordial] looks and corresponding actions of the most chearing welcome!—

*   *   *

18

Greta hall, Keswick June 4th 1819

Your letter, & present, dear Sir, ought to have [been] answered two days since: the first evening I wilfully missed, thinking to get a little more time, as the post comes late to us: and *last night*, a distressed *Lecturer on Chemistry*, (poor Man,) coming with a petition to S.

saying, if he could prevail on his ladies to attend his Lecture he could induce others to be present, took up my time again: I hope you have not been uneasy.

Your expressions of satisfaction at H.'s success at Oriel add to your other bounties: and your kind letters to H. and myself are not the least of these; you give your precious time to us, and we will appreciate the favour accordingly; at any rate, I can answer for myself.

I was not sorry to hear of poor Rich's release; H. had told me: I am happy that the widow is enabled to live without labour at her advanced age. But what shall I say about Miss Cruckshank? Our friend, Miss Barker is almost as bad; with an annuity of 400 a year, and 1200 pounds in money she is obliged to leave us, and a house in Borrowdale half finished, (the foolish building of which, has caused this temporary ruin) and retire to france to live in her Uncle's house, at Boulogne until her annuity can pay her debts. This is the precious fruits of having *a taste for magnificence*. We are sorry to part with her, and so are the Wordsworths, for she was lively, sensible, and accomplished. She taught our Girls what they Know of music, and was, at all times a great promoter of their pleasures; her pleasant Drawing-room was, at all times, when here, a pleasant lounge for Hartley & Derwent, the latter of whom, she used to keep *at Chess*, till the poor boy often declared he was much more exhausted, than if he had been working mathematical problems, or translating a difficult classic; in the same way she disgusted little Edith with Chess, who, at 11 years old could best her 5 or 6 times together: She may *now* engage with Sir

Jerry Omphrey, who is too old, and too independant to care much about *thus* passing his time. He is, however, gone to france, to retrench.

I cannot *guess* what can be the matter with Miss Brice: am glad to hear she is better: if you see her, say, I think affectionately of her and hers, for the sake of "auld lang syne". Perhaps her sister is married.

'Tis a glorious thing to have a Bishop for an uncle, if one has Sons fit for the Church; I do not mean fit, so much in point of talent, as in morals and conduct: and *I do, indeed* congratulate you, and his nearer connections on his accession to so desirable a living as that you mention; being in your own *immediate* neighbourhood.

I feel a little vexed with you, dear Mr P. for not saying *one word* about Miss E. Poole: I am always greatly interested in any account of so amiable and distinguished a person: I am told, her attentions to her Mother are unremitting: so you find she is known by her goodness as well as by her uncommon abilities. I hope Mrs Poole's health is established.

Neither have you mentioned Mrs King: but I conclude *all is well* with her from your silence.

Miss Wordsworth is, in figure, activity and spirits much as when you knew her, with a much-altered face, and, I think, an improved character: she looks nearer 60 than 50 in her profile, owing to her extreme leanness, and the loss of teeth: at Xmas, when she joined the dances of the young people, Sara thought there was something unnatural, in the incongruity of her *face* and *figure* together with her extreme agility in the dance. While Sara was feeling *thus;* her good brother was pointing out to me, with expressions of delight, the thing which Sara was remarking; but with very different feelings: Wordsworth thought these lively movements were signs of strength, and deep enjoyment, which in a woman near fifty, and his beloved sister, (for this must be taken into the account) was worthy of admiration: good man, he forgot, in the contemplation of his own pleasure, that he was addressing one who, according to his notion, must be an object of commissiration; for *I* am so *encreased* in size, that I could no more go down a dance, or climb a mountain, than I could fly over the Derwent. He, however, evidently prefers the nut-cracker nose & chin, to the full-moon phiz it must be confessed mine *does* somewhat resemble.

Southey has some thought of changing his time of visiting London & going in the early autumn to Scotland with Rickman; to town in November.

Yours was an affecting illustration of the state of those possessing a great blessing; and in *this case* more particularly so; they are on a precipice indeed! The boy thrives, but he is only 4 months old and rather delicate in appearance, though not small. S. is so fond, so anxious, and so full of directions, prohibitions &c &c he says he hardly hopes to rear him. If he die, I shall regret he was ever born! He'll be spoilt, for Sara, and Edith will do their share and the parents will do the rest. We shall *all* Spoil the darling.

Sara is still at Grasmere; Mrs Crumpe and the young Ladies have sent to beg a longer visit: she is in the same village with Mr de Quincey, who, I told you, married a peasant girl; he has two children; he does not visit any of his old friends, but devotes his time to the labours of editing a paper called the Kendal-Gazette.

Believe me, I had much rather hear of your *gains* than of your *losses*, because you can make a benevolent use of all your overplus; yet, the assurance that it does not disturb your own comfort is consolation enough.

What you say about S. T. C. is likely enough to happen; Alas, I dare not look forward: it seems to me impossible we ever should live together under a roof of our own, for we have not the means. Our separation has, on the whole, been for the best, you will easily see why. I grieve on the children's account, poor things. S. thinks Mr Kenyon will be more likely to travel than return Speedily to England. I wish he would come and take the house in our garden vacated by Miss Barker—'tis just fit for a single Gentleman or Lady. I daresay we shall soon have a letter from him. 'Tis time you should be released. You flattered me into writing so much, by saying you were interested about us. God bless you! Remember me most kindly to Mr Ward. I'm glad to hear his little pets are well.

Hartley must be now at Oxford attending the examination of St Aubyn, I hope he will come off well. I will send him your *message* as soon as I hear from him.

Yours most affectionately

S. C.

P.S. Southey shakes his head at your not coming northward; he thinks a man may find time to do anything he likes. I do not quite agree with him.—My poor sister Lovell is a complete invalid.

19

[*Keswick*] [20 *September* 1819]

My dear Sir

Mr Ward's very agreeable friends arrived
here shortly after your announcement; fortunately just on
the eve of Southey's departure for Scotland; I should have
been sorry if they had not seen him, as they appeared to
wish it so much; & as he certainly is one of the Lions
of the Lakes: for the Clerk & others are often applied to
by Strangers to point out his seat at Church to those who
have not introductions; and those who have are not a
few. We hope to see S. & his party in less than ten days;
he says, "the great canal is unquestionably the greatest
work that has ever yet been atchieved by human power."
How I should like to see it, as well as the other and more
natural wonders of Scottish land! We shall be all glad
when he returns, for *letters*, *parcels*, and persons are pouring in upon us, and you may easily believe the latter cannot be so well received in his absence as when he is here;
besides this, there is an invitation from Lowther for him
for the 23^d I suppose to be *there* when the Prince Leopold
arrives: I wish he may pass through Keswick for the girls
would be delighted to see the poor unfortunate youth, I
mean *unfortunate* thinking of his irreparable loss.

I did not like to hear that Miss E. Poole had a cough, &
wonder not at your anxiety; I hope & trust all is well with
her & you and all around you at the moment you peruse
this.

—S. T. C. is at Ramsgate with the family of those good people the Gilmans, Mrs Gilman often writes to me, C. sometimes & Hartley who spends most of his vacations with them gives me accounts of his father from time to time.

Last week I was agreeably surprized by the arrival of Derwent with Mrs Hopwood and a party of Ladies; Mrs H. had often wished to see D's friends, as well as the Lakes in our neighbourhood; I found her a most charming woman, & was highly flattered by the handsome things she said of D. & the solicitude she expressed for his future destination.

A few days since brought me a letter from Hartley; poor fellow, he is most sanguine in his hopes of success in tutorship, and thinks, his *fellowship* and *exertions* together will enable him to assist Derwent; and he assures me he will not spend *one idle penny*, keeping this laudable intention always in view. If these good resolutions last, how much I shall rejoice, as, beside the immediate benefit derived from them by his brother, it will gain him credit with all good persons and especially *those* who have exerted themselves to procure him the advantages he is now about to enjoy. He has not yet entered Derwent's name at any College, and is much at a loss what to do, the Colleges being overflowing at this time; he says as soon as term commences he will set about it in right earnest on the return of some friends to the University.

Poor Lloyd is in London, he says the noise is useful to him, his wife & family have a cottage at Grasmere; Derwent is with them at present having a few days vacation. The Wordsworths are quite in request, you have no notion how much respectability attaches to them; their society is much courted. I suppose you have seen "*Peter Bell*" and "*The Waggoner*", by W. W. How opposite is the opinion of the "reading public" upon these poems!— You kindly ask for dear little Cuthbert—he is a fine, thriving boy, not so pretty as his poor brother, but twice as large & strong, he is a doated-on darling. Edith S. is [as] tall as her mother & a fine, fair girl, very lively and intelligent & much noticed by her father's friends; she, & her cousin are much attached to each other & seldom disagree although so perfectly dissimilar in character that they are scarcely companions; for Sara is as much too fond of Study (and particularly reading) as Edith is averse to it; I *could wish* that each had a little more fondness for the pursuits of the other. Hartley always discourages his sister's erudite propensities, and tells her that *Latin & celibacy* go together; but she playfully answers, "Not the less for this, cease I to wander where the Muses haunt." Derwent encourages & instructs her; they read Tacitus, Livy, Virgil & Cicero together; and when tired of these; she turns to Ariosto, Tasso, Chiabura [? Chiabrera] & Dante.

Miss Hutchinson and Mr Monkhouse has just arrived; they tell us that poor W. is quite blind with inflamation in his eyes and cannot go to Lowther when the Prince is there, so that Ld. Lonsdale will not have any of his neighbour Poets on this occasion. By the bye have you seen "Peter's Letters"? What a rage for personality in the present day! not a periodical publication comes out but something is said upon living characters; 'tis not the thing I think, at all, to speak so much of people while they are living; in the literary gazette there was a full account of our juvenile american Scheme, and that Mrs Fricker & Mrs Southey had consented to go with the young people in their wild Scheme of colonisation.

The Bishop of London was here & his very agreeable wife: I had a mind to ask a frank for you, but I was so engaged at that time with Mrs Howly & Mrs Agnew and her party that I had no time to write, and now my motive is to tell you that your friends had been here.

Give my kind regards to Mr Ward; tell him I was much pleased to be re-introduced to his relation by wedlock, Miss Burgess; she is a sensible, agreeable woman; I saw [her] once when a little girl.

I will keep this till the travellers return, Mr Rickman will frank it.—How kind it was in you, dear Mr Poole, to tell me so much about the friends in your neighbour-hood about whom we are both interested. Poor Miss Brice is indeed a sufferer! I was glad to hear such pleasing accounts of your valuable Sister & her family; she, I think, can*not* have increased her family since I was in Bristol in 1807—she had then a sweet little girl the age of my own, and 3 sons, the youngest an infant.

I hope my dear Sir, you will *now* and *then* favour me with a few lines as heretofore; for the idea of being for-gotten by you, and thereby losing all connection with, & Knowledge of my kind Somersetshire friends is what I cannot bear to think of! You will always live in my remembrance as connected with my early wedded-days,

in the infancy of my beloved Hartley, and the *whole
existence* of that other dear babe whose name you have
more than once unwittingly given to my third son in your
kind enquiries for him, thereby recalling many, many
tender and *some* very bitter recollections connected with
his birth and death, sweet child! But I do not wish him
here.

It would affect you much if you were to see the flush
of hope & joy that spreads over the expressive countenance of poor Derwent at the idea of seeing his father next
spring! He will be 19 years old; he was 11 when his father
last beheld him! C. will be quite overpowered, and the
boy too, I conjecture, at their meeting. Yesterday Hartley was 23 years old, some days older than his father was
on the day of our marriage. I think H. is as excentric as
his father *to the full*—may he be happier!

October 3d—Since I wrote the foregoing the travellers
have arrived in safety: and I have had a letter from S. T. C.
desiring to see Derwent *immediately*—with an intention
of sending him off to Cambridge in Novr but he cannot
at so short a notice quit his situation. S. begs to be most
kindly remembered to you, he shakes his head at your
not breaking your chains and taking flight to see your
friends in the north.

Ever most truly yours

S. COLERIDGE

20

Greta hall, Keswick March 11th 1821.

My dear Mr Poole,

It was my intention to have written to you last summer, to thank you for the pains and interest you took in Derwent's trial for the Skinner's Exhibition; but was prevented by the worst news that ever reached my ears;—the unhappy affair at Oxford! It was only a few weeks since I was informed that D. had not been appointed, for having never heard to the contrary, I had flattered myself he was the successful candidate (which I am now sorry to find could not have been the case,) as the sum of £15 per Annum would have been of great use to him at Cambridge, especially as residing in Lodgings is much more expensive than rooms in the College would be, which he is not, I fear, likely to obtain. If you should hear anything of any *other* thing of this sort, I need not, I am sure, repeat how much we should be obliged [if] you would inform us how we may apply for it: Mr Monkhouse of No. 34 Glocester-place, Portland Sq would render his assistance in getting it for Derwent. Mr Monkhouse is a cousin of the Wordsworth's. By the bye, I suppose the Skinner's Ex:n will not occur again for some years to come if there is but one in their gift.

D. has [? an exhibition] at St John's, Cambridge— worth £10 per annum, and I hope he is going on well; his poor brother's misfortunes are a great burden upon his spirits at times and his father's situation in *mind*, *body* & *estate* oppresses him much but, he says, for his own individual self he feels hope, if he has health and spirits granted him to go through a severe course of Mathematical study, but nothing short of that can give him success at St John's.—You perhaps may have heard that Mʳ C. went to Oxford on H's business: the Warden of Oriel spoke of H's talents, acquirements & dispositions in terms of high commendation, but would not allow that he had been injured in regard to the *false charges* brought against him; he thought he was not regular enough in his habits to make him fit for a fellowship at Oriel; but offered him, *in the name of the College* 300 pounds (lest he should feel some immediate pecuniary dificulties,) and *to speak no more of the matter;* this his father refused, but said the matter might be referred to the young man, and if he *were* guilty of the charges in the degree they seemed to insist upon he might use his own mind as to his acceptance of the sum offered him; but, if his errors were really *multiplied* and *magnified* as he had assured him they were he thought his acceptance of the money would be wrong, if, in that case, he had not the liberty of speaking the truth. Some time afterwards Dʳ Coppleston met C. in London where the offer was repeated upon the same terms, but immediately rejected and a *Protest* against the Charges drawn up by himself, i.e. by H., delivered to the Warden, since which nothing more has occurred, for they insist on the truth of the charges and he declares he will always keep himself at liberty to proclaim his injuries, as to the *degree* of delinquincy wherewith he is charged.

H. has passed the greatest part of his time among

his friends, but principally in Bedford Square with the Montagu's, where he is translating a Greek Play, "Medea." Barry Cornwall, who was here in the Autumn, had seen part of it, told us, he thought it very well done, but he is *now*, preparing a small volume of Poems for the press. Sometime hence when he shall have given sufficient proofs of steadiness of conduct, he will prepare himself for holy orders: his letters on this subject are very affecting but it is time to release you from this unpleasant subject, excuse my having dwelt so long upon it: I should be more unhappy than I already am, if I thought you ceased to take an interest in our concerns.

*   *   *

Southey's Poem "The Vision of Judgment" is just out, a nice morsel for the Critics, if they are not tired of attacking him; you Know he is writing the Life of G. Fox, and the history of the War: S. was fortunate in meeting you in the Spring, but you did not promise to come to us; that is, you did not say *when* you would come; I think you would admire the beauties of Cumberland and Westmoreland if you could ever find time and inclination to pay us a visit. Last winter I took Sara to Liverpool, and we made a very pleasant visit at Eton, the seat of our old friend Dr Crompton; S. enjoyed the attentions she received from his large family of sons & daughters, and from those to whom she was introduced as well as the public places, which they were all eager to show her; I was pressed to leive her behind me, but I promised to send her another time when her health was more to be depended on.—You will be pleased to hear that Cuthbert

Southey, now just 2 years old, is a fine thriving child, and his 4 sisters are all well, Edith the eldest is near 17 years of age; She, and her cousin Sara are excellent friends and agree well together although of totally different characters and dispositions. I need [not] say much of our friends at Rydal Mount as you saw them last Spring—they have returned from the continent, delighted with their tour: their children are all at *School*. Does it not surprize you that such clever people could not educate the daughter, at least, without paying 60, 70 pounds a year at a Boarding School? We are obliged to teach ours ourselves. Sara is teaching 2 of her cousins music, and Latin. Edith has one pupil in music, and the rest falls to my share, with a little assistance from Mrs Southey.

Last Spring we lost our kind friend Mrs Wilson; she left H. £20—which I've just sent him. The greatest part of her income arose from an annuity: she left all her relations £5. or £10 each, and £5 to all the children in this house, just for memory. We have also lost our good friend Mr Nash: he had passed great part of the summer with us.—

God bless you!

S. C.

S. unites with us in kindest regards.

21

Greta hall, November 7th, 1821.

My dear Mr Poole

I forget whether I mentioned in my last letter to you, that Sara was engaged in a translation from the work of Martin Dobriofher, a Dutch Jesuit, twenty-two years resident in Paraguay written in Latin; it is a scarce work: the original was purchased abroad by Mr Kenyon and presented to Southey, who made much use of it in his history of Brazil.

The Translation is now finished under the title of "An Account of the Abipones, an Equestrian tribe in S. America &c. &c." of course the Translator's name is *not* mentioned; you may have seen it among the works preparing for publication by J. Murray, in the Quarterly Reviews, not the last number, but some of the former ones. Shortly after you receive this the publisher will send a copy to Stowey which we beg your acceptance of; you will peruse it with a favourable eye. Perhaps you will be surprized that [so] young a female should undertake a work of this kind; this is the history of the thing. When Derwent left School, and there was little prospect of his going to Cambridge, his uncle thought, if he could induce Murray to publish it, it might *possibly* bring some profit to him if he translated this book; accordingly Derwent began the first vol: and Sara, wishing to assist him, began the third vol: when each had done about 200 pages, M^r F's kind offer of assistance reached us, and Derwent being then at Mr Hopwood's instructing his 2 sons, it was thought too much for his health to pursue the translation, and by Mr Wordsworth's advice it was withdrawn.

When Sara found a stop was put to it, she felt disappointed, and said, she liked the employment "of all things", and her uncle approving of her specimen, said, if she chose, to finish it, at her *leisure*, she might, but she must not be disappointed if nothing was gained by it, and she must *not work too hard*.

My dear Mr Poole you must not imagine that Sara's health has suffered from too intense application to this work, for I am happy to say she is at present in better health than I have ever known her, and so fond is she of literary employments that she feels quite at a loss for her last winter's amusement; in the summer we are a great deal engaged with our friends and our amusements out of doors, that is, after the business of the house is finished, and this is not a trifle, taking in the education of the Children.—Wordsworth & his wife have just left us; he is teized with weak eyes, which make him more than ever dependant on the females of his family: he with Mr Senhouse & Southey have been on a visit at Lowther Castle, where a very pleasant party were staying, some of whom were invited on purpose to meet them.—I think I have little to add to my last letter, except that I hear good accounts from Cambridge of Derwent's improvement; he passed the two last months of the vacation at College reading with a private Tutor which was procured for him by a friend, for he could not afford to pay for it himself; his examination was creditable to him, and was the occasion of the assistance of a private tutor, as it was seen that he meant to exert himself.—Poor H. is at No. 1. Gray's Inn Square; he is preparing a volume of Poems for the press, but I fear is at a loss for a publisher; he talks of writing for present support, but *what*, and *how* Alas, I know [not]. It's impossible for me to have any peace of mind until he [is] in a regular

90

way of providing for himself: he hopes to get ordained after a time.

Dear Sir, if you should ever feel inclined to favour me with a few lines, pray tell me of your beloved niece Miss E. Poole; of Mrs King & her children; & of Mr Ward and his family: and all whom I once knew at dear Stowey and its neighbourhood, making my kind remembrance to them.

Southey & my sisters beg to unite with me in especial remembrance to yourself & I remain, most truly your obliged frd

SARA COLERIDGE

22

[Spring, 1822]

My dear Mr Poole,

Most truly welcome was your last, and very ardently-expected letter, for after reading Miss Poole's marriage in the paper, I daily expected to see, or hear from you for you had in your letter in March spoke very confidently of coming to the north with the wedding party,— and, lest I should miss you, I was miserable for weeks whenever I left the house; and always went *by the Inn* to see if I could see a carriage with a mitre on it, concluding, as Dr Sandford had joined the parties together they would travel with him. I was therefore, truly thankful for your letter, which set my mind at ease, inasmuch as I had begun to fear that something was wrong with some of you. I must now wish you joy of your new relation and join in your prayer that the happy couple may not be less happy at the end of seven years.

Sara, who is highly gratified by your approbation of her book and by the gratifying interest you express for her; smiled at your idea of "blessed singleness" for "literary ladies", without promising to profit by your advice: on the contrary, I am sure she will change her condition as soon as she can get the man of her heart—but this is a sore subject with her, dear child!—she will not, I fear, pass through this hard world without her full draught of the cup of bitterness—yet, I am happy to tell you, that just at present, she is in excellent health and spirits, notwithstanding the frequent recurrence of that most *dreadful of all* coughs: but, as it is unattended with fever, and has ceased to trouble her more than once in the night, she bears it with exemplary patience.—In the month of Sep[r] all the young ones, except Edith, were seized with the Whooping Cough; all except Sara were mildly held, but really, for a week, I thought she wd expire under every fit of coughing: after the first violent attack, I never shall forget the consternation into which we were thrown! She looked at me with terror, and exclaimed, Oh, *this is awful*! We both, however, became more calm as we saw it *was* to be borne, and a more patient sufferer than the younger Sara need not be, though the elder of that name did not evince, I am sorry to confess, an equal share of fortitude. I do not expect she will get rid of it till the weather is warmer, but n'importe; the disorder has not injured her general health—rather, I should say, she was the better for it, for her appetite is good, and she is stronger, upon

the whole than I have ever known her. This illness, and
other matters prevented her journey to town which is now
thought of for July or August; I hope nothing will prevent
her journey, yet it is very difficult to manage for various
reasons, and one is, that she cannot take so long a one
by herself—but it must be managed by accompanying
some friend or acquaintance whose time of going she must
submit to, however inconvenient.

Southey is at this moment correcting some of the latter
sheets of his "Vindiciae", an answer to Mr Butler's Book
of the Roman Catholic Church—it is a Tartar. His *Tale
of Paraguay* is much liked, and sells well; you know it was
taken from Dobrizhoffer; there is an allusion, very pleasing, to the Translator of his work, which has delighted the
young Coleridges, and Charles Lamb was much pleased
with it also, as were all the good people who kindly
interest themselves for our poor little girl. I cannot tell you
anything about the success of my husband's book, but I
see it is reviewed in the Quarterly—it is a book far beyond
my comprehension, *in parts*, and even Hartley tells me,
he means to read it three times over. H. has been writing
some Essays in a yearly publication called *Janus* published at Edinburgh—if you meet with it in your rambles
you will look at the following articles—*Action & thought.
A preface for any new work of the present day. Love Poetry.
Antiquities, Pins. Brown on Beauty.* These last five are in
succession—I am *not sure* about *Action & Thought*, but the
others I know. I think you w^d be pleased with them; the
book I hear has had an immense sale: it is the first number. He talks of publishing a small volume of Poems, and

printing them at Liverpool, but he talks of so many literary projects, which *end* [in] talk, that I never depend on his intentions. All I know is that if he do not write he cannot eat, for writing now is his sole dependance except the *occasional* reading with young men in the higher classics which does not often occur—for his School is given up for the present, and I do not flatter myself he will resume it even if pupils might be had. I assure you, I am not a little anxious on his account, for he ought to be in town to pursue a literary career, but London will not do for him! He is far too much in company even on the banks of Windermere.

Derwent is still first classical assistant at the large establishment at Buckfastleigh—at least, as far as I am at present in his secrets; for to my *great surprize*, I heard a few days since that he was just going to Cambridge to attend the divinity Lectures; Mrs Patterson said in her last to Sara, "we hope to see D. soon on his way &c &c"—I am not pleased that he has not informed me, I think it cannot be true, for I know he has no means of support at Cam: I suppose I shall hear from his father in a day or two if any change is in contemplation; he used to inform us of all his movements. I know he has had an offer to go to Quebec with the Bishop, he was recommended by the Tutor of his College, but if he were *inclined* & and if he were *fitted* for it, he is not in orders. Derwent writes in the Cam: Quarterly Magazine and has delivered some Lectures at the Plymouth Institution which were thought highly of, I suppose by his own particular friends.

Sara is, with the assistance of Edith & Bertha, making

a Catalogue of Southey's books; they work an hour and a
half each day, and they have already been nine weeks
about it: S. thinks it cannot be finished before May; it is
a most tedious employment, and very cold work, for they
have to stand in cold passages, and fireless rooms, to
mount up and down step-ladders, and the whole library—
upward of 6,000 volumes is to be arranged, so that one
set of books may be taken down and put up many times:
she is not writing anything at present—she translated another work of chivalry last winter but it will not answer to
publish it: her eyes are still [bad] and she cannot use them
much at candlelight, I should *think* they were much better,
as one cannot discern anything amiss, except she has
worked too long when they appear a little weak; still they
are not as they ought to be. Her visit to town could not be
accomplished this winter; she now looks forward to the
month of July, which is again fixed for her visit to Highgate, and *thence* she will pay several visits in town: but I
shall never believe she will go till she is actually gone: she
has never gone farther than *Rydal Mount* or *Nether Hall*
by herself. You will think me in my dotage, for I have
written this sentence *before* pray pardon it, I have written
at two different times.

My dear Mr Poole, if you visit London this spring I
hope you will try to go to Highgate to see your old friend:
Mr Gillman is removed to the Grove, I am told it is a very
pleasant dwelling. Lady B. was here last summer, and she
gave me an account of the pleasant view from the windows.
—Our friends the Wordsworths are in trouble on account
of the stoppage of the Stockton Bank:—Mr J. Hutchinson

is M^{rs} W's brother—their loss is one hundred thousand pounds! It seems the firm expects to pay all—and Miss H. has a handsome annuity left by her late brother—and the eldest Son has 5,000 a year of his own, left by his mother's uncle—and the other children are independent so that there will not be much private distress. The W's have no money in the bank. Miss W. is shortly to set off on a southern journey, and Miss Dora Wordsworth is coming to stay here, and afterwards I suppose our girls will return with her to Rydal. Southey talks of a visit to Holland again in the Spring; he is going to [avoid] his summer cold.—

How very much obliged I feel myself to you my dear Sir, for giving me so many particulars of my friends at Stowey, and for mentioning your excellent sister and her family—in your next I hope you will be able to inform me that they continue well, and if any *change* has happened, we shall know from you in due time for we do not correspond with any of our Bristol friends. It gave us great pleasure to hear such good accounts of your esteemed friend Mr Ward & his family, to these, and all around, who ever ask for us, present our united kind remembrance—to the Misses Brice our very particular regards, and I shall be happy to congratulate Miss Chubb on her change of name, if it has yet taken place. Pray tell us somewhat of your interesting relative Miss E. R. Poole—of the Cruckshanks &c and remember us very kindly to *your* own worthy houshold whose affectionate attentions to us, and wishes to see us again gave us pleasure—I cannot think of the good old nurse without a peculiar feeling of regard, for the love she expressed for my poor Hartley—

96

and for the simplicity and honesty of her own character:
—you have treasures of servants in that woman and
Martha, and I daresay I may write William in the number.

Southey sends his best and kindest wishes for a sight
of you as soon as convenient. I hope nothing will prevent
your coming and I shall think Sara very unfortunate too,
if you should happen to come while she is absent: both
of you are very uncertain in your movements, she too
has been sadly disappointed several times about going
which she wd not much regard if it were not for her eyes
which we hope may receive benefit from Mr Gillman's
care.

Cap^n Southey's book is in the Press—but it is printing
rather slowly, I believe I told you that he was employed
in the preventive service in Norfolk: he has nine children?
Mr Murray is printing a lively little volume called—"Six
months in the Antilles" by Henry Nelson Coleridge, the
youth who went to Barbadoes with the Bishop: it is very
lively: some of the proof Sheets have been sent to Southey
and Sara for their opinion. The Bishop is just married to
Miss Reynal daughter to the Dean of Winchester, and is
shortly to embark for Barbadoes.—You know, I presume,
that J[ohn] T[aylor] C[oleridge] is no longer Editor of the
Quarterly—his business in the Law encreased rapidly, but
he had *not* intended to resign the Edi:^{ship} for a year to
come. Mr M. proposed his resigning in favour of M^r
Lockhart. This gentleman [came?], with Sir W. Scott &
his daughter; he paid great attention to Sara, and told me
he had seen a picture of her, at an Artist's house—taken
for Sir G. B.—[of] which he wished to see the original: we

little then thought he was so soon to supplant our esteemed relation in his favorite employment. All John's friends are rejoiced at his release, as it was too much for him united with his profession. I wish you and he were acquainted.— May I beg the favour of you to send me Mr Cole's address, if I had known it last summer, I could have got him a dealer: you esteem him a good workman. Your last favor was directed *Kendal*, instead of *Keswick Cumberland*.

How goes our Mr Atherston? Do his Works circulate?

God bless you my dear & kind friend! Believe me ever, with true esteem Yours sincerely S. Coleridge. I must beg your pardon for the errors of this scrawl. As you are a gentleman at large you may be able to come early in the summer perhaps.

Since writing the letter I have rec^d a letter from Cambridge: to my surprize and I hope I may add *pleasure*, Derwent is again settled there reading divinity and attending the Lecture. He hopes to get a title for orders in the course of 6 or 8 months and his friends are looking out for a curacy, but he thinks it will be difficult to get suitable. Now the worst is to come! He thinks he can support himself—has *one Pupil*—hopes for more, and is writing an Essay that he has no doubt of disposing of:—sanguine season of Youth! All this keeps me anxious; he has been staying awhile with his father, who encourages him, and the Tutor of his College was very kind in his reception of him.

1823

23

Combe Satchfield, Sat: March 29–1823

My dear Sir

My nephew, Mr John Coleridge, barister, is just going to leave us for Taunton and will be the bearer of these few lines to you which I write in great haste to inform you, with mine and Sara's kind regards that if you are likely to be at Stowey this Spring we hope to have the pleasure of paying you a visit. Perhaps we shall be in this neighbourhood and at Crediton between 3 and 4 weeks longer when we shall take the Coach from Exeter to Bridgewater—it may possibly be a little longer than the time mentioned, but I hope *not* as we have been from home ever since the 6th of Nov^r.

You will I am sure be pleased to hear that our visits at Highgate and Ottery have been productive of the greatest satisfaction to all parties—I shall have a great deal to tell you when we meet, which I hope nothing will prevent: in the meantime, my dear Sir, have the goodness to send me a line addressed—Mrs S. T. Coleridge, Revd G. Coleridge's, Warden-house St Mary Ottery, Devon: and if you can receive us please to say whether there is any stage from B. water to Stowey, if not we will go forward in a post-Chaise. I prefer a *Stage* on account of our luggage which has been often wet with rain when we have travelled post—but that's a trifle, and I only name it, as preferring the stage.

Your very kind and interesting letter was forwarded to

us at Darley near Derby, seat of Mrs Evans, our very early acquaintance, as you may remember her present husband behaved to us with the greatest attention: he and all his family are passing the winter at Dawlish in this County; but we shall not have time to turn aside to see them there; Sara corresponds with one of the Ladies—*now* no longer young, but very amiable. Mr George Coleridge knows your dear niece Elizabeth; he speaks of her as all others do who know her; he is, I am sorry to say, in very indifferent health.

Sara was highly gratified by the remarks your letter contained, indicative of the great attention you had been pleased to bestow upon her labours—she will explain all, as far as she can, when she has the honour of your acquaintance.

I should not be sorry if you, and Mr J. Taylor Coleridge were to meet at Taunton; he is a man of very high character—but he is here to say, his Aunt's carriage is ready and I must bid you adieu, as I am, with Sara, to accompany him as far as Cullompton. God bless you! My dear friend, I pray that this may find you well—Sara's best regards, remember me kindly to all who remember me—

SARA COLERIDGE

*   *   *

24

At Mrs Keenan's No. 3, Beaufort's Buildings, St Thomas's
Exeter 2ᵈ May [1823]

My dear Mʳ Poole,

We received your kind letter through the
hands of our dear Cousin J. T. Coleridge whom, I am sure
you will like much on a further acquaintance—on this,
and various other subjects we will converse at your fire-
side.

We hope to be with you on Wednesday 7 of May and
the only thing likely to prevent it, that I can see at present,
is *not* being able to take places from Exeter to Bridgewater, on account of the Plymouth passengers; and as we
shall want two places we *may* be disappointed; you will
therefore conclude, if you do not see us on the day appointed that this is the case, and we will try for the day
following.—As there is no time for an answer, we must
take our chance that all is well with you—if otherwise so
that you could not receive us, let somebody be at the Inn
at Bridgewater where the Coach stops to prevent our setting off:—or, I will ask the Landlord if any letter has been
left with him for Mʳˢ Coleridge, I know not the *name* of
the Inn, but you probably do; but let us hope for better
things.

God bless you! my dear friend. Present, if you please,
my very kind regards to Mʳˢ Ward; and with our united
remembrance to yourself believe me ever faithfully yours,

S. COLERIDGE

P.S. My poor Sara is still suffring from a Cold caught in a very careless way going to Sir John Kennaway's before breakfast, in a very cold morning, neither she, nor her escort, Mr Chas E. Kennaway ever thought of drawing up the Carriage windows, in consequence of which she got the rheumatism in her head and neck which made her uncomfortable for some time—this wd not have happened if I had been of the party, but I did not go until dinner time when I perceived she was unwell. I rejoice to hear such good accounts of Miss Poole; and shall hope for good news next time from Madeira.

Second P.S.—Having been at the Coach-office since I wrote the former part of my letter, I find we *can* take places, and I hope we shall be in time for the Minehead Coach. If not, we will take a Chaise, but I beg you will not think of waiting dinner for we never care about it on these occasions: an early tea will suit us after our journey much better. God bless you.

25

[Keswick] Sunday June 29th—1823.

My dear Mr Poole,

My brother has but just informed me that he [has] not answered your letter; waiting in the hope of being able to fix his time for setting off, which I am sorry to hear he cannot at present do, as he *must* finish his "Book of the Church" which is printed as far as half way through the 2^d volume. He desires me to thank you for

your kind letter and invitation, and he will write to you
when he can see his way clear before him; that is, when
he has done some of his business in town: he will give
you, (by my desire,) as long a notice as he can: I fear you
[will] not have him with you more than a day and a night.
—You will possibly have heard of our safety from your
dear little niece, Elizabeth King, with whose society Sara
was exceedingly pleased, for she is a very sensible, and I
have no doubt when she is not in affliction, a very cheerful
companion; and your good sister is just the same amiable
creature she ever was: we are both much indebted to her,
and to every individual of her family, having passed a very
pleasant fortnight under her roof whence we were conducted to the coach by Mr R. King which we never
quitted but at nights till we arrived Rydal-Mount where
we found Hartley in eager expectation of us, walking on
the Ambleside road with John Wordsworth, to meet us.—
The next day I had an interview with Mr Dawes who appears as much interested as ever for H.'s interests, and
said his society had been a great comfort to him, but he
was not I could perceive without anxiety on his account
fearing that when he was no longer under the same roof
with him, he might go astray, for he has no notion of the
lapse of time, staying out at night sometimes hours later
than he intends. He waited until our arrival to get a place
of residence after the vacation which he passes at M^r
Wordsworth to the no small satisfaction of John and
Dora Wordsworth who are much attached to all my
youngsters, as they are to them; at the end of 5 weeks he
will live in Ambleside at a very pretty Cottage, where he

will have a large room for his School [&] a small sitting
parlour and Bed-room with board and washing in the
family consisting of a young couple with one Child and
one servant—& here with God's blessing he must maintain himself by his School & occasional Literature, but
how he will contrive to do it the first year, if at all, I am
at a loss to divine; but he has good spirits and does not
complain, yet a tinge of melancholy runs through his
writings in poetry in particular; Mr Kenyon put a Mag:
into my hands with a very doleful ditty in it of this poor
youth's: but I have seen some others of a different character, one called "*the tea table*" which is very well in its
way, and some of his partial friends say, they like it as
well as Cowper's. A Young Lady at Brathay-Hall said,
write us a poem this wet evening M^r C—— "give me a
subject"—*the Tea-table*—this was the occasion of it. Sir
Aubrey de Vere Hunt's Drama of "Julian" has been reviewed in the B. Critic by H. and he has received much
commendation for the ability displayed in it—the Author,
having heard from Mr Dawes who was the Essayist—said,
if the young gentleman was in search of a situation *as
Tutor*, in a private family he should be most happy to
have him; and as he had only 2 young Sons, his time
would not be wholly occupied in teaching—he should be
treated exactly as one of the family, and he should consider his society a great acquisition.—H. thought fit to
decline this liberal offer, and I believe he was right—if
Derwent had taken his degree it might have suited him if
Sir Aubrey would have liked him, for if he wants a man of
literary talents and attainments D. might not be amiss,

for, I regret to say, he has attended far more to *general*
literature at College than he ought to have done for his
interests at College. Derwent is now at Eton with his
cousin Edward and Mr Moutrie, late of Trinity College
Cambridge.—We were greatly pleased with meeting the
Misses Brice: Penelope is certainly an interesting woman
—if you think of it when you see her, tell her, with our
kindest regards, that Sara was very much disappointed
at *not* seeing her hand-writing in her *little book* when it
was returned from Clifton with the contributions of the
family of . . ? . . She, however, has a livelier sence of her
kindness than of this omission, and wd. be very sorry
indeed, if she did not hope to meet that Lady again, which
she [expects] to do at some future period, together with
the rest of her amiable family at Asholt whither they were
so polite as to invite us when next we visit the delightful
west country, where we also hope *once* more to have a
sight of you, our very dear, and highly-valued friend; but
not, I trust, till we have introduced you to our splendid
scenery, which we depend upon having the pleasure of
doing, at *farthest* in the summer of *1824*, so *now take
notice, if your life and health be spared until that period*
that you *must*, in this same famous Vale of Keswick, submit yourself to be a prisoner under the restraint of sleeping, eating, drinking, talking & laughing in the dwelling house of Robert Southey Esqr Poet Laureat to his
Majesty King George the fourth, situated under the great
Mountain Skiddaw, commonly called Greta-hall, otherwise "The Aunt-Hill," there to be surrounded by 3
Matrons, 5 young blooming virgins, the Lord of the Man-

sion, and his darling son, (who will then be 5 years of age) —beside three obsequious females who will brush your coat, and clean your shoes with as much assiduity, and *more* good will than you would have these offices performed in the palace of our Leviathan—well known in these northern regions by the name of Lowther Castle.—I wish my dear friend, I could give you only a faint idea of a radiant sunset which we witnessed a few evenings ago! *Skiddaw* was converted to a mass of bright Amber and a vivid double rainbow was arching the other side of the vale, which was all over of a pale green light, such as you see through one of the compartments of a Claude-Lorrain Glass: Sara has given a very glowing description of this scene in some of her letters, but I am not "good at these numbers" and shall only spoil the thing by meddling with it.—We spent a very pleasant day with the Kenyons, and I was sorry afterwards, for Sara's sake who was much interested with their society, especially K's, that I did not accept his invitation, and go prepared to stay a few days in Bath; but having fixed to leave B. on the Wed: following, I did not like to take any more than one day from my enjoyment of the society at R. Parade. Mrs K. is precisely as you described her, a very agreeable, amusing woman; but she talks a little too much to be *exactly* to my taste as a companion; still I think Mr K. fortunate on the whole in his choice: Sara thinks he might have won a *younger* Lady for his bride—I smiled at this remark but the innocent did not understand me. We were a little surprized to see Miss Curteis's marriage in the paper last week.—Sara begs her very kindest regards may be presented to you, she will not forget your companionship, nor any of the favours you lavished on us, among which was the *time* you dedicated to our amusement—Sara and Mr Kenyon talked and made their remarks about you all through the Crescent—twas well you were not there: we wish Mr K. could come and reside in the North.—The elder Wordsworths are now at Cambridge—you will be surprized to hear that John Wordsworth is a *Gentleman-Commoner* at New-College Oxford! But I believe it was not *intended*, only they *could not get him in otherwise. All here* seem to regret much that Sara could not be introduced to Miss E. Poole. Miss W. was delighted to hear us talk of dear Stowey and Allfoxden, she is a delightful companion— we staid 5 days with her 'till poor Edith was quite out of patience; she wrote every day by the Coach.

We have had several letters from S. T. C. since we saw you—one reached us at Redcliff Parade, one at Rydal to H. and one here—he improves.

*　　*　　*

26

[*January–February*, 1824]

My dear friend,

　　As soon as I had finished reading through your very kind letter, I sat down to obey your injunction to the *very letter*—i.e. that of doing what was to be done *immediately*: but you were not aware that none of my husband's nephews are *now* resident in Oxford. However,

I first wrote to Mr John Taylor Coleridge, barrister, whom you saw praying him to speak to *all his brothers*; Edward, fellow of Exeter College Oxford, may have a vote, and The Revd Wm Hart Coleridge, Student of Ch: Ch: his cousin, may also be eligible; I hope and trust, John will succeed in his applications. The Revd James Coleridge, rector of Kenwyn & Kea in Cornwall was of Oxford, but whether he is still a member of that university I know not: (Henry Nelson C— is Fellow of King's College, Cambridge.) The next day I wrote to my brother George's son —Revd George May C— curate of Shobro[o]ke near Crediton, *Devon*, and recently made Prebendary of Wells; he was bred at Ch: Ch:—after these I knew no other, but my sister wrote to S— and I wrote to Wordsworth, who mentioned it to his son of New College, Oxford, but whether any of these will be of use I have not yet heard, and perhaps they may not soon write: I sincerely wish success to Mr Stevens, especially as you, my dear Sir, take so great an interest [in] it, and on account of his becoming shortly a connection of our much esteemed friend Mr T. Ward; and I have no doubt whatever, of the merit of Mr Stevens.

I have had many things to harrass and distress my spirits since I saw you, and, I must say I felt much vexed to find that Southey had missed seeing you at Stowey; I heard of it in the midst of my perplexities on Derwent's account on his quitting Cambridge. I had only then recently learnt that he objected to taking orders at present, should not stand for an honour, not chusing to take the chance of a second rate one, and had no chance of a fellowship! Thus you see, my dear Mr Poole, there is little else but disappointment for poor Sara, and me, to say nothing of S. T. C & Hartley, the poor father is very much wounded by all this, but I hope his next letter will be written in a calmer state of mind, for poor Derwent has *now* done his best in accepting the situation of third Master of Plymouth School, from whence I have just received a good account of his health and determination to perform all the duties of the situation with the utmost regularity. He will, however, find it a very different sort of employment to the studies of a College; though he tells me he shall have leisure for his own improvement which he shall make a point of, and that having been previously acquainted with the other masters he feels himself already quite at home. The salary is 150 per annum, & he has an Exhibition or two for a few years with about 20 per annum, the income of which he must resign to me and his brother as we must, out of our little, pay his debts at Cambridge, something between 150 & 170 pnd, rather more than we expected, owing to his *not* having drawn on *that young friend*, I mentioned to you, from motives of delicacy, and never having had rooms in College—beside, maintaining himself through several vacations, a thing not calculated upon in the general way. H. says, his brother is a beautiful Classic, and might have got a fellowship at Oxford.

We have many thanks to give you for your entertaining account of your friends, and acquaintance at pleasant Stowey; I wish indeed, that Sara could have made one amongst you during that week of enjoyment—She is, at

present, dear child, a little *under a cloud*, not without
hope, however, of some bright days hereafter. She has
been afflicted for the last 6 months with a weakness in her
eyes, which, to her, is one of the greatest afflictions that
could befall her, inasmuch, as she is not permitted to use
them above half the day, so that the other half is passed
in dejection and sometimes in tears, which increases the
weakness: there is very little appearance of defect in her
eyes, so that some of her friends believe it is only nervous,
and I myself believe that if not *wholly induced*, the disorder is greatly *increased* by the state of her spirits, which
have suffered great depression for a long time past, and
I do not think she ever has been thoroughly happy in her
mind since the shock occasioned by poor H's failure: her
more recent troubles have been on D's account and in
respect to *that affair* of her own, of which I gave you a
hint in the spring, since the youth *will* persevere, and now
affects to think himself ill used: he now wishes to keep up
a correspondence as *Brother & Sister*, she has not replied
to the two last letters. Since her weakness she has played
a great deal on the Piano, instead of reading or work,
which has partly improved her execution: but she attempts no new music, for fear of trying the eyes too much.

Of Hartley I can send you a more cheering account—
he has persevered very contentedly in the School, the
profits of which nearly paid his expences last half year;
he wrote some articles for the B.C. which helped him, and
he is now writing the *Article on Poetry* for the Encyclo-
paedia Metropolitana, which, perhaps, I mentioned in my
last; it has been long in hand; but he would have finished

110

it by this time, if our neighbour at Greta bank, Mr Calvert, had not prayed him to take his son, a youth of 18, as an evening Pupil—much against all our wishes, as literary studies suit him better in the evening, and it is proper that he should walk and pay visits in the evening —but the youth is only taken till Easter. H. had many invitations for the Xmas vacation, he passed it between Brathey Hall, & Rydal mount, giving us only 2 clear days. Our cousin John says in his letter to Sara—it is a provoking thing to think that H. a man of such rare endowments, should be placed in a situation so infinitely beneath him but I rejoice to hear he is happy, and he no doubt, will find many and choice flowers, even, in his present path of life which others wd. pass unregarded; &c &c——

Sara is translating an old french Memoir entitled— Memoirs of *The Chevalier de Bayard* I think he lived in the *Reign of Chas seventh*: she thinks it more difficult than the Latin of "*the Abipones*" for the warrior terms are so numerous &c—She has done what *is* done in the absence of her Uncle, and as he has not yet read her performance I Know not whether she will succeed or not; but I daresay it will do, for she is never weary of turning to books of reference, Dictionaries, (of which this library furnishes severall in old french) &c. Many of the Chevalier's exploits were acted in Italy so that she has immense folios of Italian Histories to look into, all of which is an amusement and a thing for which she seems to have a passion: She is, however, obliged to do very little of this work at one time on account of the eyes. Murray is to publish it in the Summer, *in one volume*, not much more than one

third of the other translation; We were both highly gratified by your kind wish to see us again, and that of your
estimable neighbours, the Briceses—if we both live we
hope to have the pleasure of seeing your pleasant neighbourhood once more, but we all hope that in the meantime we shall see you here; do, do think about it in earnest.

Tuesday February 17ʰ 1824.—I began this many days
ago, but waited for S's return to finish it—he is returned
in safety; he begs his very best remembrance to you, and
desires me to add that he is very sorry he could be of no
use to Mʳ Stevens except by wishing him success; he
regrets exceedingly having missed you, and desires me to
say that Mʳ Atherstone was with him the greatest part of
the time he staid in Taunton. I have read his Poem of the
last days of Herculaneum again, and think it evinces a
very great deal of poetical talent but I do not feel very
sanguine about the Midsummer's day dreams.

What a happiness it is for all her affectionate friends,
the complete recovery of Miss E. Poole; I heartily congratulate you upon it; her life and health are very
precious to you—& the more so since you have been
deprived of your excellent young relation Mʳ S. King—
we are much pleased too, to hear that the good family
on Redcliff Parade have in some degree recovered their
spirits—your sister may, on the whole, consider herself a
happy Mother, since She has [none] of those heart-aches
that visit some of us! God bless her! She is a good and
patient spirit and deserves all the blessings heaven has
bestowed upon her, without the alloy that has been
[? mixed] with them if it be not presumption to say so

much; when you see any of that family, present our very [best] regards.—I am sorry Mr S. did not see Mr Kenyon; S. says, if he had done all that he wished to do, visited all who gave him invitations, instead of three months, he should have been absent nearly as many years.

Among the many kind, and gratifying things which we read in your letter, *the last* is by no means disregarded by us: i.e. the *good odour* that remains of us with your faithful houshold in the Kitchen—tell *Nurse*, that I told Hartley, of the continuance of her love for him, her wish to see him again, and prayers for his happiness. We unite in assuring her and Martha, that we do not forget them; and that when we turn our thoughts toward the interior of the hospitable dwelling of our friend, we never fail to see their honest faces in the back ground of the picture— in a conspicuous part of it, *next your own self*, stands your highly esteemed friend and associate T. W. (to whom, and to his amiable partner for life, offer our best regards) and lastly to leave nothing out of the scene, we behold little, conceited, shrewd looking William, and the handsome, though not over modest, poodle dog, which you used to place beside the mountain nymph at breakfast for your amusement and that of the grave Mother who presided at your breakfast table.—It is time now to release you; Sara thinks you will be as much out of patience with this small writing & thick character, as you are when your [trying] friends cross your letters; but I had much to say, & I dare not ask our good friend Mr Rickman for a frank for any but to my less able correspondents, and not always to them, so I fear—if you really should wade through this

worthless epistle you will be nearly blinded by the task.—
Pray say any kind thing to your hospitable neighbours
from us, if you should happen to say you have received a
letter from us.

O, I had almost forgot. The "Book of the Church" is
out, and rapidly going off—S. is going to print the Maid
of Paraguay, a Poem, Story taken from the Abipones.
S. T. C. has made a book about Bishop Leighton, in the
Press; and his other work—"Aids to Reflection" is also
printing.—Wordsworth is poetizing, but I know not what,
he and his sister are at Coleorton, seat of Sir G. Beaumont
—his daughter is visiting in the neighbourhood of London,
(so is Edith Southey, who, I fear will be half killed by
going out so much)—his eldest son is at New College
Oxon, and his youngest, with H. Coleridge making *little*
or *no* progress in his Studies, a spoilt Boy; rather sickly.

P.S. I have this moment got a letter from my nephew
John, he is sorry he can not oblige us by voting for M^r S.
Mr Williams was his brother fellow for years at Exeter
Col: and he cannot withdraw his interest from him. I am
quite hurt at my ill success—I hope Mr S. will get it in
spite of them all. I knew John was formerly of Ex^r and
rather anticipated this.

27

Keswick: October 17th 1824

My dear Mr Poole,

After some deliberation we think it best to
trouble you with another letter rather than run the risk
of your looking for Edith at Taunton, *now* that we have

just heard an unfortunate circumstance has occurred in the dangerous illness of one of Lady Malet's sons of Winchester School, which, by taking her Lyship and Miss Charter from that Town, will, in all possibility prevent my Neice's going there at all: for if she were to go to Taunton to see her Aunt, and Ly M. should not return thither which is scarcely likely, and has not yet been even hinted at, she would be much less likely to meet with a suitable escort from Taunton than from Exeter; and she is at this time with a Lady and her daughter who would be delighted to have [her] stay protracted to any length of time. Thus the matter stands. We are all much grieved for the poor mother who will in all probability lose her darling Octavius, her eighth & last child—we are sorry for poor Edith's disappointment who was delighted at the prospect of going to Taunton and seeing there so many of her friends: and Southey is not a little vexed, that both himself and his daughter should lose the opportunity so little likely to occur again of meeting you in your own delightful county since they cannot have that pleasure in their own still more delightful one. I hope, however, this will arrive to prevent you going in search of her, if you should have had such an intention, and I know you will forgive the trouble and expence I feel constrained to put you to.

I write on this sheet of paper* because it is the fashion in this house to do so. I daresay you have often seen our announcement of this work—I believe the author relies

* Announcing on the other side *A Chronological History of the West Indies*, by Captain Thomas Southey. Pub. 1827.

much on his brother's interest, and judges it would be useless to print a work of this nature in the usual or more common way. S. has a great dislike to publishing by subscription, but in Tom's case, nothing else could be thought of, as no publisher would risk the printing it, and he cannot afford to risk it himself—it will not go to the Press till a sufficient number of subscribers have been obtained. There is some talk of his leaving this vale, in search of some employment—something in the preventive service, if it can be obtained for a Commander's half pay, with an annuity under £100 a year of his wife's—[which] will not support a family of nine hearty children: his two eldest daughters are nearly as tall as Sara, and twice as thick, at the ages of thirteen & fourteen; they are fine, but not pretty children, except one or two of the young ones.—

I believe I did not allude, in my last, to the appointment to the Literary Society, I mean S. T. C.'s nomination to it; strange as it may seem he has never once alluded to it in any of his letters to us, nor should we have known it if Lady Beaumont had not written to congratulate us upon it. The fact is, he is, I daresay, so much in arrears, that he cannot make over any part of it to our use for a hundred a year will not be much for his own expenditure if he cannot earn some addition to it by his writings: I wish I could see the long expected book.

If you should think of it when you write pray send me Mr Kenyon's address; and I should be very glad indeed if you wd. send James Cole's address; if I had known it a month ago, I could have gained him a customer for a gold watch: was it number 3.—Mark Lane?

Now if Edith May Southey should at last after all go to Taunton how provoking it will be to miss seeing you! But it is time to release you. Relying on your kindness to excuse this letter—and in the hope of hearing from [you] before Xmas, at any rate, I remain, my dear Sir,

Ever truly yours,

S. COLERIDGE

Sara says, have you sent my very best regards to Mr Poole? And does he know how much I enjoyed my visit to him after the 3 or 4 first days? How is Carlow? does he sit up to breakfast beside Miss Poole as he did beside Mademoiselle? We were much disappointed that Sir G. Beaumont did not visit this Vale during the Summer as he promised to do: but we have just heard that he is not quite recovered from an attack of a bilious fever, and Lady B. does not appear quite well. Ld Lownsdale told S. that he did not think they had any very great pleasure in the heir—he is below par in intellect & attainments. How mortifying to a family so much distinguished for both. I always thought young B. a very dull youth, but Hartley wd never allow it: he thought it was all modesty. Ld. L. says Ly B. looks many years older than when we were at Coleorton: I thought her then the youngest and nicest looking woman of her age I ever saw: she was quite unhappy because Sara stooped in sitting and wished her to walk the room to keep her upright.

28

[*Keswick*] [1825]

Dear and kind friend,

Your very interesting letter of the 10th March must *first* be acknowledged with many, and grateful thanks, before I begin upon the *old subjects* of *myself* and *surrounding objects*: Alas, I can never repay you for this, and all the other testimonies of your unabated kindness towards us! I can only recollect and dwell upon them with heart felt pleasure! It is, indeed, a consolation to me, amidst all my disappointments and anxieties, to feel an assurance, that I, and mine retain an interest in the hearts of some whom I have known from the days of early youth to the approach of age; when I dwell upon this blessing, your image, and the scenery of your beloved dwelling place, form a very prominent part of the picture in my mind.

The whole account of your dear niece is very interesting: Southey knows the Bishop by Character: the family are highly respectable: Wordsworth believes it is of *ancient* respectability from the name, and he told me his reason for thinking so, but I shall mangle the thing if I attempt to write it, it was something about an *inscription on a Gate* —n'importe: they are decidedly persons of talent: I heard a great deal about the controversy, and Dr. C.— of course we were, at any rate Southey, was on the side of the master of Oriel. The gentleman who is looking forward to the happiness of becoming a connection of yours was considered a reading man at Oxford, and during the latter years of his residence, very strict in his religious duties; the prospect is a good one, I need not say our best hopes and wishes are for the happiness of the parties, and that you will always have reason to rejoice, if the union should take place. I wish somebody wd send me a Somersetshire paper that I may read [of] the marriage, and thereby be able to calculate when it is likely we should have the pleasure of seeing you in the north; for, I fear, you will be too busy to afford us a line. However, I intreat you, when you are really on the wing, to write either to me, or Southey, from the next town—the town next to us—you stop at, that we may not be out of the way when you make your approach. Our friends often do this, or we might *chance* to be out of the way, which would, in this instance *in particular*, be truly mortifying: as we sometimes go to Rydal Mount and sometimes to Nether-hall, the seat of Mr Senhouse, and sometimes, we are out for the day, upon the Lake or Mountains.

Sara and myself have just returned from spending a pleasant month at Rydal Mount—the worthy inmates often talked of you—W. always gets into a worry when he talks of your having never *yet* afforded us a visit: (while I think of it, I *must* tell you that if you come by Kendal, your next stage is Ambleside, the beauties of which you must see, and a Mile further on is Rydal, where are two fine waterfalls, the Lake, Rydal Hall, Rydal-Mount, &c all which will be shewn you by the Wordsworths they being in their immediate neighbourhood; but I cannot help feeling a little jealous that the

W.s will probably see you first) which he thinks you could so easily have managed. There we saw a great deal of Hartley, who happened to be at leisure part of the time, as it was the Whitsund holidays: he had the grace to come every evening almost, after his school recommenced, but I am sorry to say he does not visit our worthy friends as often as they, and I wish: I am surprized at this, since Mr W. and his family are the persons, of all others, in that neighbourhood with whom H. can be at all upon an equality in point of companionship, now that Mr de Quincey is intirely out of sight. Sara enjoyed her visit much: Dora Wordsworth is a very affectionate, sensible, and well-bred damsel, much attached to S. and Edith, and fond of having them at Rydal, especially as her father, who cannot bear her absence for many days together will not let her stay long at our house. Miss W—— (my friend) is as amiable and kind-hearted as ever, and takes as deep an interest in all that concerns us; you will, no doubt, be glad to see her again, and to be introduced to Mrs Wordsworth, who said, "I *quite long* to see that Mr Poole here whom you so often talk about." On looking over yr. letter again, I fear there is little chance of your coming *this* year, as Mrs Poole has not been dead more than a year in August.

My husband's book, so long looked for, is at length advertized—"Aids to Reflection on the formation of the Manly Character &c. &c." by S. T. Coleridge, Hessey and Taylor. He has another work, on Logic, in hand, which we expected to see first.

I hope my dear Mr P. that you received the Copy of

"Bayard"—the Publisher was directed to send it to Skinner [?] Street with proper address: we have not yet heard much about the sale of it: Murray said, in a note a month since—"Bayard goes on well"; he has shewn some interest for Sara and has sent her books at different times as presents.

Southey is in Holland at this time, we have had one letter from him, he will stay a month, and a few weeks in town on his return, and in the last week in July will, we hope, bring home with him his truant daughter, who has not returned to us with her sister Bertha, who has now been with us a Month,—she was tired of so long an absence from home, and thought an interval of 14 months enough for so great a distance: to be sure there is some difference between the ages of 16 and 21—but I confess, I did not expect that Edith would have extended her absence to nearly two years, as it will be by the end of July: she will think Keswick a dull and rustic place after living so many months among such gay people: she tells her cousin, she shall quite enjoy the quiet of home, and enjoys the thought of seeing us all once more.

I have not heard from Derwent of a very long time; he was far from well when he last wrote; had been writing a few poems, which by the way, he would not let me see because, forsooth, I had dissuaded him, while at Cambridge, from indulging that luxury, and had not praised his productions. I hear he has delivered a [lec]ture at the Atheneum at Plymouth, on Poetry, chiefly Wordsworth's, and [it was] thought well of by some; I doubt not, however, there were two opinions, though I, as his mother, only heard one. I am rather anxious when he does not answer either mine or his sister's letters, lest he should be prevented by illness, or the dread of communicating ill news.

Cap^n S. was much pleased by your very friendly remembrance of him, I gave him your name, and that of Mr Acland as you desired: he and his family have just left this country for Cromar, Norfolk: where he has an appointment in the preventive service.

[The] Southeys (Southey and his daughter) met S. T. C. at dinner at Sir G. B's previous to his departure, he looked well and was in good spirits—Sara had a note from Ly B. a little before telling her that her father had been often in Grosvenor Sq—and that he had finished his Essay for the R.L.S. which we were glad to hear. We have a few friends in town, who, knowing how seldom that gentleman writes, when they see him are so good as to send us a report of him: among these is our good nephew, J. T. Coleridge, who is now the Editor of the Quarterly review. —My dear friend, I do not like to make you uncomfortable by alluding to any of my troubles and disappointments, but after the concern manifest in your letter respecting the health, spirits, and general welfare of my dear girl, I cannot conclude this poor letter without telling you, what you will be sorry to hear, that her eyes are very little stronger than when I last wrote; her spirits are better *on the whole*, though, if I were to say that she was "as gay as a lark", I should make a very bad simile— very many things concur to press her spirits down, but I do not quite despair of seeing her if not as happy as she deserves to be, at least, in a state of mind to bear those evils which she cannot avert, with tolerable Cheerfulness. Happy would it have been for her, if she had been born with a less sensitive disposition. She has an invitation to pass the next winter in town but I believe she means to decline—she cannot enjoy visiting till her eyes are better: hot rooms, late hours and excitement of every kind are bad for her. She unites with me in the kindest remembrance and thanks for your wish to see us again and joins with me too, in kind regards to your excellent neighbour Mr Ward. Remember us to the Brices when you see them: Sara wd much like to see them again. Remember us to poor old nurse if she be living, and to Martha. Southey was much pleased that you and his Aunt, liked each other so well. God bless you! Believe me, your attached friend

S. COLERIDGE

Regards to all who are so good as to enquire about us.

P.S. Sara thinks, by what I have said, that you will imagine that her papa never writes to us: he does write much oftener than before he saw his daughter, but he is long in answering our letters; when we wish an immediate return we address our inquiries to Mrs Gillman who never keeps us in suspense.—Southey's "Tale of Paraguay", from the Abipones, is published; Sara corrected the last proof sheet of the Latin Extract after S's departure: he is writing a reply to Butler's Book of the R.C. Ch: he has other things nearly ready for the press. W. is about to publish some Poems, he wishes Murray to publish for him, but I am not sure how that matter will be setled.

When you write, pray tell us somewhat about our friends the Kings. How goes on the fair damsel, Elizabeth by name?

29

Keswick October 12th [1825]

My dear Mr Poole

When this letter reaches you I hope you will be quite free from the illness which you laboured under last winter, and when you have a leisure half hour to spare it wd give us all great pleasure to be assured of it from your own hand: in person, I would have said, if I thought it were of any avail: still I do not despair—everybody comes to see the Lakes, at least, once in their lives, Mr Poole would have some of the best guides in the country in the company of the northern bards; he would have five or six attendant mountain nympths, (who would, perhaps, tieze him a little in pointing out the different beauties of the scenery) to go over the highest hills with him, and the Matrons of the houshold would employ themselves diligently, either at home, or at the mountain's base in preparing refreshment for the return of the wanderers. One of these nymphs will shortly be in your county, and I write just at this precise time to inform you of it, as I think, if you went to Taunton during the few days she has to stay in it you would like to shake hands with her, and I know she would like excessively to see a person so highly esteemed by all her family, and one whose name was so often mentioned by her aunt & cousin

after the Southern visit. Edith is at this present time at
Ottery for a few days, she will return to Exeter and I
believe, will go to Taunton about the 18th of this month,
stay with her aunt Mrs Mary Southey, till the 25th and
then proceed to Town with Lady Malet who is, with the
Miss Charters, at the residence of Mr T. C. near Taunton.
I do not know whether Edith will go to Lynchfield at all
or not, I hope she will not be there at any rate, if you
should favour her with a call at her Aunt's.

We heard of your illness in a letter to Sara, from dear
Miss King, brought by Mrs Barber who favoured us with
a call and tea visit: she told us at the same time that you
were perfectly recovered, since which, I have not been
able to hear any tidings about you; but I am willing to
believe that *no* news, is *good* news, in this instance at least,
though it has not always proved so to me ——

You will be sorry to hear that Sara has not lost the uneasiness in her eyes, and that she is obliged to abate a
great portion of her former studies, although she has not
wholly given up all her favorite amusements. She has
finished "Bayard" and it is half through the press, (she
is correcting a Proof sheet at this time) but I suppose Mr
Murray will not bring it out in the winter; you will perhaps see it announced in the next "Q.R."—it has been
announced in some of the periodicals already. I wish I
could, as *certainly*, tell you when her father's work will
appear; I have often seen it announced, as "preparing for
the press", but that is all: "Aids to Reflection" is the title.
I hear from Mr Field, late Judge advocate at Australia,
who has just seen him, and brought us a letter, that he is

looking extremely well, & is *"as wonderful as ever"*. Mrs Gilman's bad state of health has obliged her father to put off her visit to Highgate, she, (Mrs G.) being obliged to live almost constantly at the Sea-side; she is now, I believe, at the Isle of Wight and when she returns, it will be necessary that her sister should, for a time, reside with her to perform all the houshold duties for her, and thereby, occupying their only spare bed, it is not possible for S. to be there. They hope the next Spring will afford an opportunity of her being with them, and Mr G. thinks, if nature in the mean time do not cure her, he shall make every effort in his power for her relief, by consulting some of the best occulists in her case.

Her newly married cousin Mrs Patteson wishes to have S. with her, but she can have no enjoyment till her eyes are better, especially in the winter, as she is obliged to avoid the light of the candle, and hot rooms are very distressing to her: she danced in a party a few evenings ago, and it had a visibly bad effect, making the eyelids look *red* and swollen, which is always the case when she is much heated by exercise: she is very thin at present, but is, I think rather better on the whole than she has been for many months past.—M^{r} & Mrs Guilmarde have been here for a fortnight at lodgings; they brought a letter from Mr Kenyon; they spoke of the great pleasure they had had in your society at Stowey: I think them a very agreeable pair.—Southey has had a very severe cold which lasted 3 months & left him in a weak state: thank heaven he is now in a better way, in excellent spirits, and hard at work: the 2^{d} vol; Peninsular War—is in the press,—Life of G. Fox—Maid of Paraguay, a Poem from Dobriz^r and many other things are preparing for publication: writing for the Qly—and letter-writing take a great deal of his time: and occasional absences a little; he is going for [a] short time to Lowther-Castle, for having refused so many invitations since he was last there, he is now obliged to go.—M^r & Mrs W. are with their eldest, (only, I should have said) daughter in Wales, where they tell me, they found Mr Monkhouse in a very bad state of health, and looking dreadfully: his complaint is a derangement of the stomach.—Miss W. is as young as ever, in regard to her love of rambling over the hills &c—she, with a party of young people, have been passing a week at Miss Barker's deserted house in Borrodale—Sara was with them and on their return some of them remained a few days here.—R. Lovell, and a Son of Mr Hill's (Southey's Uncle) passed a month here in the Autumn, and we had Mrs Keenan from Exeter with us & Mrs Clarkson a few days: we were disappointed in our expected visit from Mr Henry N. Coleridge who, I am sorry to say, was prevented coming by illness; he is going to Barbadoes with his cousin the new-made Bishop who sails the 1st of November.

My dear friend I sincerely hope you will, when you have time to write, be enabled [to] give us a good account of Miss E. Poole, (if her name is still Poole) tell us also some [thing] of our interesting friends at Asholt; of Miss E. K. Poole, of dear Mrs King and fam[ily] and remember us very kindly to all these—to all whom we knew at dear Stowey but in a very especial manner to our highly respected friend Mr Ward. We desire to be kindly remembered to good old nurse, and Martha, if she is with you, with good wishes for little, consequential William.—John Wordsworth goes on steadily at Oxon: during Hartley's vacation he read with him when he was not at Keswick; H. has helped him a good deal; but now that he is pretty hard worked with 14 pupils in his own School, his Uncle & M^r W— think it is too much for him to read at night with John: the younger son, Willy, is at his school, but an idle boy. H. works hard & cheerfully, and does not *appear* to look back on what he has lost with any regret, except for the severe infliction of suffering on his parents, his brother & sister—and the appearance of ingratitude to those excellent people who assisted him in his education. Poor fellow! "What did Mr Poole say about *me*?" enquired he, when speaking of you; he looked relieved when I told him, that your censures were mild, and your good wishes I was sure, not withdrawn from him; but, I added, it must be difficult for one constituted as Mr P. is, to account for such a line of conduct.—Derwent is going on well at Plymouth; his sister is in despair at the cruel distance that parts them; she wishes *so much* to see him. He passed his summer vacation at a very pleasant house, the Lady of which was a mother to him, & to whose son, an invalid, he was tutor for the time. I tell him, he must save all the money he can, to bear the expence of a journey to the North, or to help *us*, if we take a journey westward to see him and our other dear friends in that direction, in w^h. case how delighted we shall be to look in upon you once more.—Sara begs me to say, with her highest re-

gards, that she hopes you will accept of a Copy of the
Chevalier, the good Knight whom she is quite enamoured
of, and to ask you, if she is to direct the publisher to send
it direct to Stowey, or will you have it left anywhere in
town for you? Sara will be glad to hear that Mr Atherston's poem has pleased the "reading public" but she does
not expect it. S. thought it was not likely to please, being
all descriptive: there is good poetry in it, but it is less interesting than the others. M^r & Mrs Field from B. Bay,
are a very interesting couple; the Lady very young and
pretty; she has been at Rio Janeiro, Bahia, and other parts
of S.A.—they took care to tell me, on the first visit, that
they had read the "Abipones" through with great pleasure, and the gentleman added, if Mr S. himself had translated the work it could not have been done better. I am
glad such things as these have not turned my poor child's
head: her Aunts say that her brothers are quite enough to
spoil her if she had no other flatterers:—but what are her
attainments, or her virtues, when compared with those
of your dear niece? I shall rejoice to hear that she is quite
strong & that it is not impossible that she & S. may live to
see each other.

And now it is quite time to bid you farewell. I am vexed
that I was out of the way when Ld. Lowther called yesterday, I might, possibly, have got a frank: I do not fear that
you will care for postage, but I am always glad when I get
free postage for my unworthy egotistical scrawls.

G. C. would have given us his vote, if he had *then* been
M.A. but he put off going to Ox^d—till a few months ago
for *that* degree: he is my correspondent since his p or

Mother broke her arm. I rejoice that Mr Stephens got the living, without my aid, at any rate. God bless you!

S. COLERIDGE

Kind love to Mrs Chester—did Tom Chester die, when you wrote last he was at the point of death!

30

Keswick, August 28—1826

My dear friend

If the late events of our house had been of a cheering, instead of a distresful nature, I should not have remained so long in silence towards you but I have had numerous letters of sad necessity to write during the last 6 weeks which has obliged me to defer those which will be as welcome late as early, not being of a nature to give anything but pain.—Six weeks ago, my poor brother Southey followed to the grave his fourth dead child! If you had known the blooming Isabel,—you would have uttered the same sentiments which, in the anguish of your regret, escaped you, when the beauteous Julia died! I not only recollect the sense of the words, but the look and attitude in which they were spoken! Marks of sensibility like these endear the manly character to my memory, I can*not* forget them although 28 years have heavily rolled on between. My poor niece was only a fortnight ill in a sore-throat: her father had returned from the Continent about a week, and we all hoped she was recovering until the last day, when she was pronounced in danger! She was almost fourteen years of age.

130

I wish my dear Mr Poole I could be quite sure that you were quite well at the moment you are reading this; for, so many of our friends have suffered during the late hot weather, that I cannot open a letter without dread! All in this house have been indisposed, partly, indeed, owing to surprize and grief they have endured! Poor Mrs Lovell has been a severe sufferer!

Now, I would fain finish in a cheerful strain; but first, for a few more distresses which the benevolent persons who correspond with me are doomed to read.—I believe I told you that Sara would go to town in the spring of this year for several months—she is not yet gone. We had not been able to meet with a proper companion for her, for almost every one travels partly by night which she cannot do, as sitting long in a carriage induces a most violent uneasiness in the back and loins; at length she was engaged to go with Mr Gee in a sort of Barouche, and he said, he would take all possible care of her, staying on the road at different friends' houses at Kendal, Liverpool and Birmingham. The day had long been fixed, and it proved to be only 10 days after her cousin's death. She wrote to him at Lowther and gave it up, for she was quite disordered and would not be persuaded to go—he then said he would wait a week longer for her, which was so great an advantage that her uncle insisted on her going. Accordingly she went as far as Kendal, and I went with her so far; she was so weak from repeated sleepless nights, that it was impossible to proceed—and I brought her back, since which she has slowly recovered, but her disappointment is so keen that all here are of opinion, that if she is suffered to remain here all the winter brooding over the impossibility of her being able to take the journey, that it will have a bad effect upon her health as she grows daily thinner—and looks almost as white as this paper— so I, *under advice*, have resolved to go as far as Darley Hall—seat of our old friends M^r & Mrs Evans, n^r Derby, where she was invited to stay when she came to town; remain a week with her there, and take the chance of a companion for her from thence: this is rather a strong measure for *me*, but we think that as life is uncertain, and after 50 an ailing man may soon be carried off, if she goes not *now*, and waits at home all this winter, she might not see her father again, as he might be in a state of health not to admit of her visit to him, beside other reasons, strong reasons, which would be tedious to you to repeat.

Now, my dear Sir, I have thought continually of you in contemplating this announcement, but as we have not heard from you, I think there is no chance of seeing you at Keswick this summer, if there were, and Sara were *not* here, how would she for ever regret it! I cannot tell you how much she values the pleasure of your society and how intirely she is capable of appreciating the worth in any character with whom she is associated: so that I am selfish enough to almost wish you may be coming next year instead of this—but I dare not breathe such an unworthy thought in the presence of this family—so pray, do not betray me for the world! Wordsworth never comes here that he and Southey do not rave about your never coming to the North. I hope I shall live to see the day!

Were you surprized to hear that Southey was really

returned for Downton? All was done when he was at
Leyden—he means to vacate his seat at the sessions—in
the meantime he receives his letters free—and is *R.
Southey Esqr M.P.* until then; but he will not frank letters,
although, it seems, he might do so. I shall be very sorry
when he is no longer M.P. for my daughter's postage is
rather more than I can well afford, although many of her
friends get franks—especially the Coleridges.

I shall be at home again before the end of Sep^r—nay,
in the second, or third week I shall be at Rydal-Mount
whither your letter may be sent, gratis, so please dear
friend, pray afford me a few lines if possible—I should
like well to get a letter from you while staying there, and
it would delight them to hear about you. Sir G. & Lady
Beaumont will be in that neighbourhood about that time,
they are going to Lowther Castle, where W. now is; he
makes frequent visits to the great man who always invites
our Bard, but he is so devoted to his desk, and dulce
domo, that he will not often go. It answered well his
going to Holland, for he missed his cold.

I wish I could tell you good tidings of H. & D. the
former is a sad loiterer in the land: he will *not* put his
shoulder to the wheel, and I have no hope that he will
ever maintain himself wholly—and if not, what will be
the consequence? His father wishes him to write something with his name, but a few Essays is all he has the
resolution to finish. He has just sent off some of these to
A. A. Watts Editor of the Literary Souvenir, who applied
to him, and to his sister for contributions, this is all he has
done lately. He was here for a fortnight: and when I am

at Rydal, I must look out for a cheaper home for him than the one he now occupies, for he is much in debt, I hear. Derwent is waiting with great anxiety for a curacy for orders; his poor father has been much harrassed by his endeavours to help him, and has not yet succeeded: I know not whether he means to return to Cambridge where he was all the winter.

Sara and Edith, Bertha & Catharine are talking over the merits of the morning visitors just departed, with much eagerness, as they are strolling on the Lawn as I sit and write at an open window. The Archbishop of Dublin and his daughters are here; he might have offered me a frank if he *can* frank for England; if the Gen: Peachey were at the Island, I would trouble him with this letter, but he and his family are travelling in scotland, so, I conclude I must trouble you by post.—God bless you, dear Mr Poole! believe me ever truly yours

S. C.

N.B. Send me Mr Cole's address. *Watchmaker*: and Mr Kenyon's address.

How is Mr Ward, that man of many daughters, and an *only son*, which is bad for that son if I may judge from what I see going on here! Cuthbert is a sweet child, but who can stand the united indulgence of papa, Mama, and 3 sisters, besides an old Nurse's. Remember us kindly to him, and tell us how the Kings go on at Bristol, and if the gentle Elizth is still in the bosom of her family. How are the Brices—the Cruckshanks and above all, tell us of Mrs Sandford. The fair Eliz^r Muscomb Poole, and all of your name—how are they—please to remember us to them—and do not forget to name us to good old Nurse, and Martha, and William—and give Carlo what he likes best, at your next dinner hour for the sake of "Auld lang syne." You see I presume that all remains in statu quo.

How provoking it is that I cannot get a frank for this worthless epistle! S. T. C. is writing another religious work—he tells me, he has had a number of letters from Clergymen on the subject of his last: & many visits from them. Have you read "6 months in the West-indies"— Henry Nelson Coleridge's work?

P.S. Since writing this letter, we have rec^d one from Wordsworth; he says, the Archbishop of York, and the Attor.-General are at Lowther Castle: the latter informed him of the base behaviour of Wakefield. Do not think the worse of us when I tell you that some years ago Wakefield and his father dined here. If you have read Coleridge's last work—"Aids to reflection"—you will see mention made of Dr Magee Archbishop of Dublin: he is a great Theologian; with him is a most intelligent young Irish Clergyman, Mr O'Sullivan; he almost worships Southey—he is a most eloquent as well as truly pious man; he has spent every evening here for a fortnight and Southey walks with him, or rows with him and the girls upon the Lake most days. Sara is not a little gratified by his frequent quotations from her father's "Lay Sermons", which he seems to have intirely learnt by heart. He likes the ancient Mariner.

31

[*Summer*, 1827]

My dear friend,

Sara informs me that she has had the pleasure of seeing your niece, Miss C. King, a few weeks ago, in town—you were well, but she was sorry to hear of the death of your good cousin, Miss H. Poole:—will not her loss be much felt by Miss E. P. her niece & Protegée? She had also the good fortune to get a glympse of you in December, which I was glad to hear, as she was absent when you made your flying visit in the North. I daresay you were much gratified by the handsome manner in which our friend got into the Atheneum—I hope, as most of my husband's nephews are members, that if Mr Kenyon should reside in London they will become acquainted. S. T. C. tells me that his nephew Henry Nelson C—— has written a Pamphlet, in which his, (S. T. C's) opinion on the Catholic question is stated, "but unfortunately," he says, "he has not stated all the grounds &c"—I have not yet seen it. There are a few verses in the first number of "the Standard" by S. T. C. Southey liked them much.— For the last month my sister Lovell & myself have been alone—Southey and his whole family are at Harrogate with Dora Wordsworth—her father has also been with them:—they had *all* been somewhat indisposed, & S. hoped to escape his grievous summer cold:—it has, however, I am sorry to say, found him out there—the rest of the party are better, except poor Mrs S. who felt *sure* before her departure that mineral waters would not "administer to a mind diseased," to much effect: Edith tells me, her mother *is* better in spite of herself. Since their departure I have received the Gold-Medal, by the kindness of our fr^d Mr Senhouse; it is very handsome. Dora W. is still in a very delicate state of health.

I daresay you heard of our loss in the death of our much valued Sir George Beaumont. Sara has been often with Ly B. in town, who bears her great loss with fortitude & is, in her state of widowhood, S. thinks more interesting in her manner and conversation than ever: they were alone, for the most part, and her company was most edifying to Sara, who has no objection to religious readings & conversation. Ly B. was obliged to be in town in her business of sole Executrix to her belovèd husband's Will. He was so good as to leave me £100 in his Will—the same to Southey, and to Wordsworth £100—and an Annuity for life of one hundred pounds! Was not *that* a handsome remembrance? I fear poor C— w^d feel a pang on hearing these, and no mention of his name—but Sara, who was present at Highgate when my letter arrived there announcing the thing to him which I thought myself in duty bound to do he expressed no sentiment but sorrow for the loss of his esteemed friend! I find W. does not wish to have his Legacy spoken of—so—entre nous—Ly B. told Sara, that Sir G. meant to have made some additions to his will, if time had been allowed him: she has written to S. T. C. to tell him how much she has been amused & instructed by his "Aids to Reflection."

Since I saw you at Keswick, my dear Sir, I have never

seen one of my own *immediate* family. Hartley is still at Grasmere, *always promising*—and Derwent, I am glad to say, is *performing*, very industriously at his Curacy at Helston where I am told he gives satisfaction to his parishioners, who have acted very liberally by him in the collections of the first Easter dues, and other matters, & numerous Matrons exert themselves to be helpful to him in getting into his house, which, poor fellow, must be but a meagre affair, as he cannot afford to furnish more than the rooms in which he sleeps & sits, when he has time *for* sitting, (for he has a very heavy duty) and a room for his servant, & the kitchen, all of which must be done on credit of which he has had but too much already. He says, Helston is a delightful climate. I am looking forward with hope that I shall see my dear girl again in Sepr or October, she is at present with her father, but is going to spend a month with M^r & M^{rs} Ed Coleridge at Eton. She has been quite well during her absence, & likes London much.

July—the former part was written some weeks since, but I thought I wd not trouble you with it till after S's return. I am sorry to say he is still in the full enjoyment of his Harvest Asthma, as his strange summer cold is termed; he looks very thin and his poor apprehensive partner is far from being on a bed of roses, she thinking him worse for his journey rather than otherwise. They had very wet weather during two days of their homeward journey, & he, with Bertha, who drove him in a Poney Chaise, got wetted to the skin twice over in each day. S. however, takes it patiently: he is a little anxious at present about his brother, whose employment in the preventive service will soon cease, and there is no prospect of any other for him. You have doubtless received his book before this,—I have nothing about the Sale of it.—Miss S. of Taunton was delighted to see you, she takes a visit from you as a very great favour,—and we think a letter from her a great favour also, at her advanced time of life.

We expect to be a little gay, *for us*, next week—the W.s are coming to us, & Lord Colchester, and his son are coming to spend some [time] at K.—but we are disappointed in the expectation of haveing Mr Chancey Hare Townsend, and his interesting wife in this neighbourhood for 3 or 4 months, owing to the delicate state of health of the latter . . ? . . had taken a delightful house for them on the top of the Hill—going out of the town, on the left hand side, you passed it on your return. Mr T. was a great friend of Derwent's at Cam: he is a poet, and has just published a Satire, without his name, called, "*The reigning Voice*":—I told S. this morning, I did not think this Poem wd ever have been produced, if Pope had not written his Essay on Man. S. only nodded—C.H.T. is a great favorite—but I am not *quite sure* that S. likes the Poem.

If providence had not ordained it otherwise, we should have had Sir. G. & his dear Lady with us at this time, a pleasure I had look^d forward to with great desire: her Lyship is so good as to wish to have Sara with her at Coleorton, on her return to the North; that cannot be, for she must come down with some friend and if she were left at Coleorton, she would have no escort the rest of the way homeward, 200 Miles.—My dear friend, if you should be inclined to favour me with a few lines some time or other, let me know somewhat of Mrs Sandford, of Mrs King & her family, and of the Brices, Cruckshanks, and my old Stowey friends & acquaintance, but most of all of yourself.

My daughter tells me there is a new edition of her father's poems now in the press, with additions, alterations & omissions, in short, a selection—I hope it will sell pretty well. You did not, in your letter to my brother, say you had seen Hartley at Ambleside, so I am afraid the interview was a painful one: he expressed himself in a letter to me, much gratified in seeing you again, but said, he hardly could muster courage to present himself before you: he had not appeared to Sir George Beaumont a few weeks previous to your visit from a consciousness of insufficiency—&c &c—poor, poor Hartley!

God bless you my dear Mr Poole—excuse this egotistic epistle—and believe me ever your truly obliged & sincere friend.   S. C.

Finished July 24th) I had been thinking I would keep this letter for my Lord Colchester to frank if he shd. offer —but on second thoughts, I think I must reserve that chance for a letter for Derwent as he is the poorest man of the two: in this decision I *know* I shall have your sanction: I have just got a letter from him: he tells me that he shall be at Exeter for *Priest's Orders* on the 13— i.e. yesterday, and will return to Plymouth next day, and on Saturday in the Steam-Boat to Helston. He never was in his whole life half so actively employed as now, and never was so happy. That's *one* comfort at least for your poor friends: for his father as well as myself have much anxiety on his account yet it [is] *bliss* compared with the other unhappy business. Excuse my mentioning this again: tis time to be reconciled to one's miseries!

32

Keswick, June 2, 1828

My dear friend,

Perhaps, before this reaches you, you may have heard, that Edith Southey is at this time with the Misses Charter, where her father, if all be well, will join her about the last week in June, or first of July, & that they hope for the pleasure of spending a few days with you, if they should be lucky in finding you at S. about that time. Southey left us on the 20th May for L. where he will stay 3 weeks; thence he will make a few excursions in the neighbourhood of London and then proceed to Crediton, Taunton, Stowey, Bristol &c &c. and if possible we shall see them both at home in the end of July, though I rather doubt the possibility of their return so soon, as they talk of a tour through Wales.

My poor sister, thank God, is somewhat less dejected than when you were here; but a little in gloom at her husband's and daughter's absence: it is the first parting since the awful event of this time two years.

It was very good in you to recollect me at Wells—I was most thankful for your letter; but do not think of a frank when you feel an inclination to indulge me with a few lines, for I need not say how much it gratifies me to be assured that you sometimes remember us. A thousand recollections, half pleasing, half painful are connected with you, & the scenes around you; and I have a sort of melancholy satisfaction in the intercourse which is kept up by our occasional letters, to say nothing of the regard I feel for your friendship, independant of these, and for the kind interest you express for us. Mr Sandford has, indeed, been fortunate in so soon obtaining the Bishop's favours, and I am pleased to hear it, inasmuch as it is matter of satisfaction to you on account of your excellent relative, Mrs Sandford. Mrs S. has a letter from her husband, who is able to walk about town at the rate of 12 miles a day without fatigue, he has seen a vast number of persons, amongst which are Sir W—— S—— Sir R. Inglis—and the Wordsworths who are at present in L.—he has seen John Coleridge & Henry Nelson Coleridge —but I believe has not yet been able to go to Highgate: before you see him I hope he & S. T. C. will have met. Coleridge has just published his Poems in 3 vols: a selection of the early poems—with many new ones, &c &c. You know he has lost his worthy brother, George, he died in the winter, before his death he dictated a kind letter to his brother Samuel, written by his son—he w^d have liked to have seen him before his departure. Col: C—— has just left London, he pressed his brother to go to Ottery, & it is settled that he is to go thither accompanied by Henry in the Autumn. You kindly mention the happy pair at Helston; my new daughter is eager to see all her husband's relations, but when Sara & I are to have the pleasure of seeing them both, cannot at present be known. They will break up their School for the vacation, on the 11th of June, and if Derwent can get a Clergyman to supply his place, they will spend their holidays at Ottery, Plymouth, and Exeter: a little recreation will not be amiss for Derwent who has at present a very great deal both for his head and hands to get through, but as he is in good health, all *that* is as it should be. Hartley is going on much as usual at Grasmere, writing a little, but not half enough for his expences, which, nevertheless are moderate: he is, just now with Mr Professor Wilson, at his pleasant summer residence on the banks of Windermere: he wishes Hartley to return with him to Edin:h in the Autumn, and stay at his house all the winter, thereby getting into some regular employment of his talents with a view to his more regular support—he intends to go with this kind friend if he can manage to pay his debts for Lodgings &c &c—he says, "let not my dear mother entertain vain fears, authorized [by] the past—the *past is past*, —allow me to consider it as but the . . ? . . history of another man—*only* in my progress to be remembered, as having relation to myself." Be it so. But alas, I cannot but feel misgivings,—I confess, I am afraid of Edin:^r—all his friends, however, think he ought to go—heaven grant it may be for good!

Sara has been, on the whole, in good health since her return. Her marriage is, I suppose, very distant, for her cousin is young in the Law, and though it is thought that he may pass a brilliant career when his talents are known, it must take some years to establish him, and the friends of both are solicitous that they should not settle until an adequate income is insured. There is nothing but patience for them.

* * *

33

My dear friend,

The few lines that I am necessitated to write to you by this post, will, I am sure be most unwelcome to you. Southey informs us, that it will be quite out of his power to visit his friends in the West this summer, and that his daughter must either join him in London, and return to the North with him in July, or, look out for an escort for her journey homeward direct from Taunton.

I wish, my dear Mr Poole, I had known of this change before I wrote to you—lest you should have made any sacrifice of other engagements in the prospect of seeing my brother and niece at Stowey. Southey does not seem to be aware that you had been informed of his hopes of seeing you, though it was agreed between us, on the eve of his departure, that I should write to you and therefore, he will probably not write to you on the subject which determined me to give you this unpleasant information. I hope, however, if anything should take you into the neighbourhood of Taunton that you will give Edith a call, though, possibly the residence of the Misses Charter may

be some miles from Taunton and quite out of the route
of your other engagements: she informs us that as soon
as the weather is better, she is going with a party, to visit
Linton & Linmouth, and Minehead & Dunster—would
this trip take them through Stowey?

I hope, my dear Sir, you will soon be thinking of a
journey to the north—in the meantime I trust I shall
either, from Edith or yourself, hear good tidings of you:
and now, as I have no news that I did not communicate
in my last I will say, farewell, with the usual remembrances to enquiring friends and an assurance that I am,
ever, with great regard,

most sincerely yours,
SARA COLERIDGE.

P.S. We have very cold weather, with daily rain, and
all the vegetation is extremely backward—Edith com-
plains of the weather in yr part of the world.

If you should see Edith pray give her Mrs Cole's
Address.

34

Keswick July 15 1829

My dear friend,

You are very, *very* Good, indeed, to think
of us amidst yr. numerous & interesting engagements—
and your letter, which though sometimes hoped for, but
not expected, gave me great pleasure, inasmuch as it con-
vinces me that we are still regarded by you; and that *you*

are not only free from any of the more corroding cares of life, (this I *presume*, from the tone of your letter, and judging from existing, *apparent* circumstances: for I am convinced unless a Man is a *parent*, an unhappy husband, or, in abject poverty, he cannot be *very* unhappy—that is to say, if he have, as I am sure *you* have, a healthy body, and sane mind) but in the actual enjoyment of many valuable blessings:—and although you *may* count years 7 times 8, I see no reason, nor do I despair that you will not enjoy them to a very protracted period:—be that as it may—I rejoice to hear of you as you are.

Your account of S. T. C. was better than the one contained in a letter last morning fm our excellent friend, Mrs Gillman: you must have met him in a lucky hour— she says, he has been a great sufferer of late, and has rallied at intervals of short duration only: he has been obliged to keep much in his room, even at Meals, & for the present, has given up his thursday-eveng. parties—she says, be assured we will take all possible care of him, but every species of excitement must, for the present, be kept from him, for fear of encreasing the tendency to erresipelas that Mr Gillman so much dreads. This account of her father has distressed Sara greatly, and added some weight to her present anxieties respecting the approaching change in her condition, separation from her dear, & most highly-valued friend R. S., her beloved cousins, poor Hartley, the Wordsworths,—her Aunts, *all;* this most delightful land of her birth—and last, not least, I guess, the parting with her Mother, by whose side she has lived, (with the exception of a year and a half's absence in the

South, and a few occasional months absence beside) for more than 26 years, and being an only one, she has been to that mother, almost *more* than a daughter. In the month of Sepr her cousin, H. N. C., if nothing should happen to prevent, means to join us here; and they are to be united at our parish Church of Crosthwaite, and then proceed to a lodging in some one of the vales, perhaps Grasmere, for 3 or 4 weeks—before going finally to town, where I am sorry to say, it seems her lot to dwell; which w^d be no matter of regret to either of us, if she were a strong woman, and had not such decided habits fitting her for a quiet life in the country. A Barrister's wife sees but little of her husband, so that Sara will be transported from a *too* bustling family, to one of utter loneliness, except from occasional visitors—she thinks she shall find plenty of employ, and amusement, for her leisure and I pray that she may find it so. The Lawyer's vacation lasts 6, or 7 weeks in Autumn, which, in many instances is spent in the country. If they have their health, and his business encreases, all will I hope, be well—he is very rheumatic at present, or rather has been so this spring— and is just, only, convalescent. Perhaps you know that he has resigned the Sec-Ship, to K. C—— it was calculated by the Committee, that 2 Sec's—could not be afforded, in w^h case Henry could not remain, as it wd take up *more* than the whole of his time. This resignation has been a great grief to me, and occasioned great opposition to their immediate union, on the female part, but we gained nothing by resistance, and the thing is, it seems, to take place, relying on an increase of business, and on the

being made Reporter to the New Court of Equity next
year which w^d fully compensate for the loss of the S-ship
to the new College. After their departure, as soon as I
can get away, I am to go to Helston, for a *long* visit—
where I shall finally settle I know not, yet; D. & his wife
say my natural home is with them—time will shew:—at
my age, perhaps, it ought not to be matter of *very great
moment* where the time is past between the present and
the last home—but old age is full of doubts, fears, and
cares, unknown to earlier years. Derwent & his wife are,
now, in London—Henry speaks highly of our daughter-
in-Law, and says, his Uncle was much pleased with her—
at Highgate—I am anxious to see her and the dear child,
and heartily wish I may be in a more tranquil state of
mind, than I am at this existing moment.—

Southey, and his family are just returned from a visit of
5 weeks, at Mr Senhouse's, Nether Hall, Cumberland—a
fine old place wh: I believe I have dated from in former
years. It is near the Sea—& the party, 7 in number, have
benefitted greatly, by the visit except Southey, who has
the Hay Asthma since his return in all its virulence. You
do not mention it,—so I conclude you have not seen his
book: Sir Thomas More—or—Colloquies—by R. S. I
think you w^d be pleased with it.—I believe Coleridge's
Pamphlet has not been published—as I remember Henry
said once—"my uncle's work is waiting till he is better"—
did he say—it was *printing*?—Southey is much annoyed
at the C. Emancipation—I have the greatest dread of the
subject—especially as Sara, the only one in the house, is
rather on *your* side of the question—she, in general, sits

silent when the matter is discussed, but at Rydal-Mount where we were staying for a Month in May, she talked much with W. who is equally strong against the measure, with Southey—but he will listen to another side with more tolerance, and there, I heard a little on both sides. You will, perhaps, wonder at my cowardice in not reading this part of your letter to Southey; but the fact is, he always is so much affected by the subject, that I am determined to keep it out of sight now that the papers have in some degree become silent upon it.

Mrs Sandford is right in teizing you for a visit—I hope she will succeed—tell him, says Southey, that he did not call on us last time—we shall all be most glad to see you, and I hope you will be here when we are not quite so full as we are soon likely to be. All the world are coming to K. this year I think—I like our Autumns much better when they do not all come at once. Pray give us a line when we are likely to have the pleasure of seeing you. I believe I told you in my last that my two sisters in London had left off business—one of them is coming here soon for a long visit—the other is going to Whitby. One of Mr Hill's sons was here all the winter. My dear Mr P. you do not say anything of the Cruckshanks's—I suppose they are as usual—& the Brices. Poor Mrs Chester will leave but few descendants considering her numerous family originally—I think she had, in all 9 or 10 children. Is Miss Roskilly still single & her cousins the Misses Poole? Miss E. K. Poole how is she? But if I have the pleasure of seeing you, we can talk over all our old friends! You are very kind in wishing to [see] us at Stowey—I hope to see you

at that pleasant place once more before I die—but I shall
not be able to tarry anywhere on the road when I am
"stepping westward" in the Autumn or rather Winter
which it will nearly be before I shall get away. I am in
some hopes of a friend to accompany me in the journey:
I sometimes hear of our friends the Kenyons—I should
like well, to see them again—especially the gentlemen.

Hartley is just now on a visit with Mr Professor Wilson
at his country house on Windermere at 6 miles from
Rydal-Mount; he has been there for the last 8 weeks and
I understand M^r & Mrs Wilson have invited him to stay
as long as they remain in the country. I am sorry I cannot
say that he is exerting himself as he ought to do—for he
is much in arrears with his lodgings and tradesmen. When
we were at the Mount we saw him most days: I am in
despair when I reflect upon the state of his affairs. John
Wordsworth has a small living given him by Ld Lonsdale
nr Whitehaven—his aunt, Miss W., has been dangerously ill at his house in Leicestershire.

Remember us most kindly to Mr Ward & to any of our
old friends who may remember us, and above all to M^rs
King and her family.

God bless you, my dear Mr P., believe me, most
sincerely yours,

SARAH COLERIDGE.

All our circle write in very best regards to you and will
be delighted to see you when you can come.

Southey bids me say—that he expects to see you for a

longer time, when you come northward—you saw nothing of the country, and we saw little of you.

Pray excuse blunders, there are plenty.

I kept this in hopes of a frank: but the General is so much in requisition here that I cannot ask him for another—& as Derwent is the poorer Man I must only ask for him. You will understand & agree to this, I'm sure.

35

Rydal Mount: Saturday Sept. 26. 1829

My dear Mʳ Poole,

You will, I trust, pardon me for so long delaying my thanks for yr. most kind letter and invitation to myself and our excellent friend Miss Trevenan; who, by the bye, knows a little of Mʳˢ Sandford, having met her, I believe, at Clifton: for which reason, as well as on other accounts, she laments with me, that it will not be in her power to tarry in Somersetshire after she has paid her visits at Clifton, but must haste into Devon with all speed to see, I believe, a sick relation; Miss Trevenan is gone to Stow to see that place, and the Boltons, so I cannot hear the detail of her reasons for *not* being able to grant herself and me the indulgence you offer us: for when we talked it over, she was very decisive, which is what I chiefly recollect—being, as you may easily imagine, in much confusion of mind as well as circumstances, on the eve of our departure from dear G. Hall.

Unfortunately, too, we shall leave Bristol about the 16th

151

or 17th—which wd make our passage through your neighbourhood happen at the time you speak of as being engaged; i.e. from the 18th to 25th, so that I could not see
you even for an hour, unless you happened to be at B.
water on your journey. Miss Charter has sent me an invitation, which I must also decline, which I am sorry for,
except on this account, that I am far from well, and perhaps the sooner I reach Cornwall the better it will be for
me and Miss Trevenan, who wd be in ill luck if she were
forced to delay her journey on my account a single day.
She is, however, all kindness and has won all hearts, by
the extreme benevolence of her character.

I have little doubt, however, that I shall get well on the
journey; and while—I stay in Bristol with yr dear sister
which I hope to do during my friend's stay at Clifton:
she purposes leaving me on Radcliffe Parade about the
8th or 9th and will take me up again in 8 or 9 days after
to proceed on our journey.

We leave this sweet spot on Monday Morning for
Chester where we stay 2 days—thence through Wales to
the Menai Bridge, &c—I hope Miss T. will avoid Liverpool, for I could not pass through that town without a
visit to the Cromptons who have been for 33 years such
inestimable friends to me and mine. I believe I shall not
be able to tarry at Ottery at all.

Thank you also, dear friend, for your good wishes—
the young folks are very happy at present—they passed
the first week at the rural Inn in Patterdale—the 2d at
Rydal Mount—the third at Keswick where they will continue 2 more weeks, and then proceed hither for a last

look at the Lakes and Mountains; and they will, by that time, have the Bard at home who is now making a tour in Ireland with Mr Marshall, M.P. for Yorkshire.

Henry is quite enchanted with all here—and full of thankfulness for the manner in which everything was conducted to do them honour on the important day, which happened to be fair, *all through* for a wonder; Mr John Wordsworth performed the ceremony—Mr Southey gave the bride away—Mr Senhouse with his 4 young ladies, (bride's maids) Genl and Mrs Peachey with my sister Martha and all our girls, making 8 brides maids including Dora Wordsworth. Miss Trevenan &c. accompanied them to Church in four Carriages all private over which was a saving of expense to us; (Henry brought a Carriage with him from Lancaster, which his brother-in-law, Mr Patteson has spared him for the time he stays) after Church—a very elegant breakfast was ready prepared, in part, on the evening before, under the superintendance of Edith and her sister, in Mr Southey's Study, which went off well, and at one o'clock the separations began—the pair, for Patterdale the rest for Derwent-Water bay, the present residence of Mr Senhouse, where a dinner, Ball, and supper was given and they separated at 4 the next morning. Do not suppose that I went to this merry meeting: I remained at home with my poor sister Lovell, and, even, began some of my packing, such as books, which was better than sitting quite still, and thinking of the miseries of quitting a beloved residence of 29 years duration which, you will see, by this date I have just undergone.

The rain is pouring down in torrents, what a sad time it is for the country: luckily for us it was a lovely day on thursday, and Miss T. enjoyed the beautiful drive from K. It was fair too, all day friday while she visited Coniston: we expect her to dinner, to stay here till Monday.

Mr S. and his family w^d have been glad if they could have detained Mr R. King awhile with us, but he was obliged to go, only giving us one evening: he asked me to stay in Bristol on my way, I could not then promise, but have since written to Mrs K. I shall not be able to receive her answer, but I shall take my Chance.

My dear Mr P. I have indulged in scribbling to you an account of the Wedding day, more for the amusement of yr young cousins and Miss Roskilly if you shd take the trouble to say you have heard from me: pray remember me most kindly to them and all my Stowey friends, and the Misses Brice when you see them; and with M^{rs} & Miss W's, and my united best regards, believe ever, most sincerely & gratefully yours,

S. COLERIDGE

Mrs Gillman writes us, that S.T.C. is a good deal indisposed. Derwent took down from London to Helston a son of Mr Montagu's as a private pupil, a Young Man.

36

Helleston, June 25th–1830.

My dear friend,

Last year you gave me a most kind, and cordial invitation (including in it my excellent travelling

companion & conductress Miss Trevenan,) to pay you a
visit at Stowey: will you be equally glad to see me this
year? I flatter myself you will if you happen to be disengaged at the time of my journey through your country.
I purpose leaving Helleston about the 2d week in July,
& I mean to go straight on to Bridgewater *if you can
receive me*, if not, I shall accept some invitations I have
had at Falmouth & elsewhere; but I wd. infinitely rather
pass the intermediate time of my journey to my daughter
at Hampstead, with you, than with my more recent
acquaintance; all of whom, it must be acknowledged, have
paid me very great, & kind attentions.

My son & daughter-in-law, with their child & servant
left this place last week for Plymouth where they will pass
the vacation with the Pridham family; Mary is to use the
Bath, she, I am sorry to tell you is in delicate health, and
Derwent has been an invalid ever since an attack of bilious
fever in Feb: he will, no doubt, come back to his duties
quite restored, and we are not without hope that his wife
will regain her strength in her visit at her native place
under the care of her good mother: but as I hope to see
you soon I will not trouble you with a long letter, leaving
all adventures of my own, and all queries respecting yours
for future conversations under your hospitable roof. If
you can receive me I will write again as soon as I receive
your answer as possible, waiting only for a letter from my
daughter, who is, at present, on a visit at her cousin Ed
Coleridge's at Eton.

Have you yet seen yr friend, S.T. Coleridge's last work,
a small volume on Church & State &c—? if you have, you

could not fail to know the portrait in one of the Notes: I was much pleased and affected by it: more of this hereafter if I am happy enough to be able to see you at Stowey; (if *you* can have me, I hope nothing will happen in my own circumstances to prevent,) we will talk of this & many other matters.

In case I go to Stowey, will you have the goodness to tell me if there be a daily Coach to Stowey; I shall go in the Coach from Exeter, and I remember when Sara & I visited you, we arrived an hour or two before the Stowey coach set forward; I mention this to spare you the trouble of another letter; and if you should be disengaged during the latter weeks of July, I shall esteem myself very fortunate. I had not the least idea last year that I should be travelling your way, this; but Sara wishes me to be with her at her expected confinement, which will take place at Hampstead, (by the blessing of Providence) where her husband has taken a small furnished house: they have been offered a house at Windsor for 3 months by Dr Keate (the canon house) but I set my face so much against their accepting this favour that it has been given up, to my great satisfaction.

Dear Mr Poole—I have a hundred questions to ask about Mrs Sandford Mrs King and family, my kind entertainers last October; Mr Ward and my other friends in your neighbourhood: but if I am to see you soon, it is best to leave all these things that your precious time may, only, be taken up in your answer by the necessary replies: and I will now only add, that if you have occasion to absent yourself from home occasionally during my visit you

need use no ceremony with me, or, (I am about to take
great liberty with you) if I should fix on a time for reach-
ing Stowey when you may happen to be absent I shall not
mind being received by your Servants, for, to say the
truth, I must leave Helleston at the time fixed, because
Miss Trevenan will have written to her other visitors who
are to succeed me here: I think I shall leave either on the
13th, 14, or 15 of July, and shall be 2 nights on the road
so that—but I think it be safer to trouble you with another line to make all clear.

God bless you! I remain yours affectionately

S. COLERIDGE.

37

Helleston July 14–1830

My dear Mr Poole,

My plan of being with you at the end of this
week, has been frustrated by various accidents which I
will explain hereafter—and, as you kindly say I may
suit myself as to the exact day of my arrival I have ventured to fix on Tuesday the 20th for the commencement
of my journey, and shall be at Bridgewater on Thursday,
hoping to find a place in the coach to carry me on to
Stowey. I need not say, my dear Sir, if you should be engaged on that day, I can take care of myself.

Our excellent friend Miss Trevenan, (if I will stay here
till *Tuesday* the 20th,) has proposed taking me in her carriage to Truro, sleeping at the Inn, and seeing me in the
Coach, the Regulator, for Exeter on Wednesday morning

—this will save me from going to Falmouth & staying all night at the Inn, and setting off at a *very early* hour in the morning; the Coach passes through Truro at a later hour and will take me up there, the place having been taken from Falmouth which can be done by letter. Now, the Regulator goes only 3 times a week, or I might manage to be with you a day sooner, but I trust it will make no difference.

Miss T. wishes for tidings of her friend Mrs Sandford, these, I shall be enabled to give her when I have seen you; she was much gratified by your polite mention of her; she never happened to meet you in your visits to M^rs & Miss Poole at Clifton which she regrets.

—I, now, see nothing to prevent my being at Stowey by the 22, (Thursday;) if illness, or anything should occur, we must each let the other know by letter—and I think it will be best, (if you *can*, conveniently, do so) to speak for a place for me in the Minehead Coach, so that no Bridgewater passenger may step in before me, I say this because it *may* come in full from other places or, it may, for all I know, start *immediately* from Bridgewater, in that case I have a better chance of a place.

I have written in a bustle, just setting off for a country visit—pray excuse the rigmarole I have penned, which, I hope you will understand, and believe me, my dear Mr Poole—

yours very sincerely

S. COLERIDGE

P.S.—Miss T. means to visit in the neighbourhood of Truro, and if possible, bring back Derwent and Mary when she returns as they, also, will be visiting in the county after leaving Plymouth. D. must return sooner than at first intended because of the members being in Helleston.

38

1—Downshire Place, Downshire Hill, Hampstead. Sunday Sepr. 12. [1830]

My dear Mr Poole,

As this letter will, I hope, conclude with a happy announcement, I venture to promise, it will not be wholly uninteresting to you; nor will you, I am sure, be sorry to hear that my journey was much less irksome than I had anticipated. At Bridgewater an elderly female, who should have been an outside passenger, entered the coach, with many apologies from herself & the Innkeeper, which I assured them was quite needless: she proved an accommodating fellow-traveller, and during the whole of our journey to London we continued mutually pleased with each other. Her history, which she gave me in her best, though, intirely, unsophisticated language amused me greatly; and if ever I should stay in her town, a thing not very likely, I shall call on Mrs Towells, widow of the Master of a Coal vessel, who some years since was washed overboard, leaving her a youngish widow with 9 children, all of whom she has decently brought up by the profits of this said vessel: she was going to London for the first time in her life, to see her eldest daughter, who 7 years ago went as a milliner to town, and now is first shew-woman at one of the fashionable houses of business.

At the White-House, Picadilly, I found my son-in-law's

Clerk, who put me into a coach—and I found myself at Downshire-Hill before the young couple had risen, which Sara was a little annoyed at, not expecting me so early. I found Sara in much better condition than I had even hoped, though not without all the minor annoyancies of her situation, from the thraldom of which she expects to be relieved in the course of the next week. I was sorry not to see Mr Ward on the morning of my departure—[his niece, Mrs Woolam, has not recognized us here; her dwelling is seen from our windows, if she still lives where she did 3 years ago, when Sara called there to return her visit to her, and Miss King had accompanied her when she was so good as to call on her at Highgate. Perhaps she may be from home, as many of the dwellers here are gone to the different watering places. Say nothing, (if you please,) of this to Mr Ward.]*

Soon after I arrived here I sent the little parcel I had brought for Mrs Stutfield and received a polite note from her in which she intimated an in[tention] on the part of Mr Stutfield to call on Henry; but as he lives 10 Miles off there can be no intercourse; I like *her* very much. M^{rs} & Mr Gillman were here this morning, and have taken Henry away in their carriage to see his uncle, who is very poorly at this time; I have not yet seen him, but as soon as he is well enough, after his daughter is safe in bed he will come over. I hope to see Southey here in the late Autumn, which will be a real pleasure; Dr Southey is going to run down to Keswick for a week if possible; the Colonel, Henry's father, and his daughter are at Keswick,

* This passage is diffidently crossed out in the MS.

160

and a great deal of other company; we have had nice letters from Greta hall. My dear Mr Poole, I shall be much obliged, if you will give me a few lines after the next confinement of Mrs Sandford, whose safety I shall be glad to hear of; and be kind enough to mention the little treasure at Fairfield and her interesting Mama, with whom I was so much pleased in my pleasant visit at her house. Tell me of the Wards, the Butters, and of Mrs King and family, to whom I beg to be kindly remembered. Since my arrival here, Henry has been home to Ottery, where he was for some days, ill, with inflamation in the eyes; his wife was anxious for his return yet dreaded the journey for him, by night: he came, with bright eyes indeed, but with considerable pain in the back and loins which has continued more or less ever since until now, so that if the D^r is to be fetched in the night, he is the gentleman that *cannot* go two Miles in the night. Luckily, the parish Clerk of this Chapel lives close by, and will go, at any time for us, which, as we have no man-servant, is a great comfort.

You were quite right in y^r conjecture that these modern houses, though small, had not *very low ceilings*—on the contrary, they are almost disproportionately high: this is a great little dwelling, and we should all be well satisfied with it, if it afforded *one more* room. The view from the upper rooms, of London, is quite delightful, and Hampstead is quite as pretty a place as it was described to me by Miss Ward. I have had the honour of a call from the Misses Baillie, Joanna is a very first-rate person—two other families have called, and we are not sorry that *only* two have done us that honour, for Sara is loth to be seen by strangers in her present condition.

My old friend, Mrs Calvert, late of Greta Bank, has taken lodgings next door to us, in order to be near us: this is a great pleasure, she poor soul is an invalid, she is scarcely able to walk from her own door to ours so crippled is she from rheumatic pains. I will now bid you adieu for the present.

Lest I should forget, when I close my letter, I beg to say, when you see Mrs Ridler, that I regret not having seen her during my pleasant visit at Stowey; I am sorry, also, to have missed a sight of Miss Roskilly, and beg my respects to her. William is an excellent Charioteer, and conducted me very carefully to my destination at Bridgewater; I desire to be remembered to *all your hous*[*hold*] they all contributed much toward my accommodation when under your hospitable roof.

We have, at present, a great deal of Mr Henry's company, and hope to have him at [home] for upwards of a month longer; I reckon he will be rather dull when his wife is confined—she takes an almost daily drive with Mrs Calvert which is very useful to her, but she has not yet been incapable of walking daily a short way.

Sepr. Since writing the above Mrs Burgess, & Mrs Woolam have paid us a visit: the former was going to Bristol & took letter from Mrs H. N.C. to Miss E. King. The Woolams are gone, for 2 months to Brighton. I was much shocked at hearing the dreadful account of Mr Huskisson's death! Mr William Hazlitt has also taken leave of this world—his career has not been of very long duration, that is to say, he has not reached the period of old age: I suppose he is not *much* beyond 50.—I have received a very satisfactory letter from Miss Trevenan, giving an account of the Grammar School Examination, in which she says, Derwent has established his reputation as Master & she has no doubt his school will rapidly increase: she has many opportunities of hearing the different opinions, beside those given by the examminors, as she is acquainted with all the first people in that part of the county. Mrs Fisher & Mrs Marsh were in D's house for some days, and Miss T.'s house was also quite occupied: there were many dinner parties in the town, and a Ball at night. I believe I told you, that neither Derwent or his wife attend these balls; they *could* not, if they wished it, as it would not be proper to leave the house.

October 8. Yesterday forenoon, about 11 o'clock Sara was safely brought to bed of a boy who, with his mother, is going on well. He is about the middle size, a little more than 8 pounds in weight. All parties seem satisfied with his appearance, but his father thinks he [is] too much like himself to be pretty; he *wished* for a girl, but is too happy at the well-doing of his wife to care, very much, about the sex of the Child for she is *better than could have been expected.* I wrote in her room & she has just requested her kindest, best regards to you. Poor father at Highgate, has been very nervous about her, he will be now, relieved; for Mr Gillman will have carried him the good tidings yesterday; I have not yet seen Mr G. to day, but am anxious to do so, to know how he has taken the long-

163

expected news. God bless you, my dear Mr Poole! Believe me ever most sincerely & affectionately yours,

S. COLERIDGE

P.S. A long letter brings me the news that John Wordsworth is to be married on Monday the 11th & on the 20th W. & his wife & Daughter are going to Trinity-lodge for a month, & afterward to London, so we shall have the pleasure of seeing them here. Pray excuse blunders.

39

1 *Downshire Place, Downshire Hill, Hampstead.*
August 16th 1832

My dear friend,

We wish, much, that we could have seen Mr Stutfield after his visit to you, as we might, thereby, make enquiries concerning your health &c &c—which might have spared you the trouble of a letter, which I shall be anxious to receive as I have no [opportunity] of hearing of you, at present, by any other means: I say this, because we heard through poor Mrs Woolam, many weeks ago, that you were indisposed; most glad shall we be to hear that your health is re-established.

Mr S. no doubt informed you of the increase in this family: I am sorry to add that since he favoured us with a call Sara has been much thrown back by an attack of Influenza. From the affects of this by the blessing of God! she has nearly recovered; and on Thursday last she, with a small party, took her babe to Church, where it received

164

the name of Edith; and, what will perhaps greatly surprize you as it did all his friends, the grandfather came
from Highgate to be present, and to pass the rest of the
day here!— — You have probably heard that S. T. C. has
intirely left off the use of Laudanum; he has suffered
greatly by the effort, and has been confined, almost
exclusively to his room ever since; but since he has resumed the use of the Sulpher-Bath, he has rallied somewhat, and is at present in less pain and less sick than usual,
and able to walk up and down the garden once a day.
His power of continuous talking seems unabated, for he
talked incessantly for full 5 hours to the great entertainment of Mrs May and a few other friends who were
present, and did not leave us till 10, when he was accompanied home by the Revd James Gillman, (son of his
friends,) who performed the ceremony, and when Henry
called to see him yesterday he appeared no worse for
the exertion he had made.

Coleridge talked a good deal of you, as he always does
when he speaks of [his] early days; he told me to let him
know when I obtained any news from you. In speaking
of Miss Wordsworth I did not tell him of the present
uncertain state of her health, and that her anxious friends
scarcely dare hope that she will be able to pass another
winter, because I feared the news would throw a damp
over him immediately: nor did we once allude to the
circumstance of his son Hartley's removal to Leeds for
the same reason, but mean to conceal it from him till we
can better judge what the consequence of it may be.

Dear Mr Poole—you have always taken so kind an

165

interest in our family concerns that I scruple not telling you
anything that occurs to my mind when addressing you.
The change above alluded to is always uppermost in my
thoughts. You know, for the last 12 years, almost ever
since poor H's great misfortune he has resided in the Vale
of Grasmere, a place the most desirable for him, in his
very peculiar circumstances; for he is known, from infancy, by all the Vale—&, I may add, spite of his errors,
much beloved & cared for by his many friends there, at
the head of whom stand the worthy inhabitants of Rydal-
mount, who say, they have been with the Mistress of the
house where he resided, and she will only lett his apart-
ments with the condition that if he wishes to return to
them they must be instantly given up, for she is quite sure
he will never do in Leeds, and she w^d much rather he had
remained with her & her husband, [as] they are used to
him and could put up with his want of punctuality which
may make him an uncomfortable inmate to strangers who
do not understand him. The history of his removal is this
—a gentleman of the name of Brigley [?] who is writing the
history of the "Countries of Yorkshire and Lancashire,"
to come out in 12 monthly numbers at 5s. per number—
sent part of the copy to Hartley requesting him to read
over and revise his work, and send it back each month for
the Press, for which he offered £60. H. sent back the first
number in due time, but the second was not ready—
whereupon, Mr B. takes a journey to Grasmere intreat-
ing H. to return with him & be at his house, for he is now
dissatisfied with his own part in the work, seeing his re-
vision, (which, the W.s say, was an almost intire re-writing

of the whole,) and asking him to be the Editor of it with his own name. H. made many excuses, but was at length prevailed on to go back with him and he has since sent for his books and other things and means to stay for 2 years. The Prospectus of the Magazine is altered, and H. is printed as the Editor to my great annoyance, for I am quite sure he will tire of it before he reaches the 5th number. He tells us in his letters that he now writes 8 hours a day, that Mr B. is more than satisfied with his performance, & he hopes we shall be reconciled to his change of life when we see the result. He thinks it was his duty to embrace an offer which wd render him independant at least for two years—and he cannot but feel satisfied with himself for having had the resolution to make the trial. He would infinitely rather be in Westmoreland than in Yorkshire, but he has made a sacrifice of inclination to Duty!

All this wd be very well if he ever fulfilled an engagement of this sort in his life; but it appears to me, and Henry thinks so too, that, if he had even so much resolution, the writing 8 hours a day is beyond his physical powers—if he [fails] the thing falls to the ground. Mr B. did very wrong in forcing the engagement upon him for he might have guessed that a man of H's abilities & education wd not have been living where he found him but for some very particular reason, he, therefore, should have been better informed before he took such a decided step.

Excuse, dear friend, this long detail—but as poor H. is your godson, and as you loved him so much in infancy, I cherish a hope that you are still interested for him, and for us, on his account. I have now a favour to beg—you said when I was last with you that you had a few things of S. T. C.'s writing if I understood aright. Henry is preparing his Uncle's poems for the press, in a cheaper edition and is collecting everything he can to add to the Vols —could you have the goodness to spare us what you have by you—it w^d be a great charity—we hope that something may be made for him, for, of course, he must, "sorely want it."

Colonel Coleridge is in a very weak state at present, he wishes to see all his children—the Pattesons are at Ottery, and John, the Sergeant in the neighbourhood. Frank is his neighbour & James, the Cornish Rector, is going home when he is well enough to travel after an attack of Erysepelas—our Henry is the only one, (for Ed. and his family are at Sidmouth) at a distance: he is to leave us for the paternal abode next monday, so we shall be left alone in this land of Cholera, which increases the disorder under which we both have suffered for the last 10 days—namely a derangement of the interior which has thrown us into the Doctor's hands, but I do not fear the Cholera for myself.

Mr Ward, who with his family I hope is well, must have had much anxiety for the fate of his niece, Mrs Woolam, who we are told is still in a very uneasy state—Mrs Burgess has been staying with her, but as her disorder was scarlet fever we have not visited her, or even sent to the house; we see Mr Woolam in passing the door once or twice a week.

I hope, my dear Sir, you will be able to give us a good

account of Mrs Sandford her husband & family and pray say how many children she now has—she had 3 when I was at Stowey. Has Mrs Acland any other little one than the darling I saw at Painfield?

I beg to be kindly remembered to all my Stowey acquaintance, if they ever ask for us, particularly Mr Ward and his family. If Mrs King is with you present our very kindest, best regards. Believe me, dear Mr Poole, ever sincerely yours

S. COLERIDGE

P.S. The Southeys were all tolerable when I last heard from them—but our good old friend Miss W. is so much out of health that her friends do not expect she will be spared to them through another winter! Henry is appointed one of the Registering Baristers, which shortens his visit at Ottery. I was much disappointed that Sara & her husband could not have the pleasure of visiting you last year.

40

13 *Richmond place, Brighton October* 18 1832

My dear Mr Poole,

Your most friendly letter containing an invitation to my son-in-Law Henry N. C. ought to have been answered sooner, but when you see the date of this, & when you know why we are here, you will excuse the omission. Our poor Sara is reduced to a very sad state of stomach & nerves by over-nursing; and her disease, which, by the Medical-man is called Puerperal is of the most distressing kind. She was failing in health & strength even before her husband's visit at Stowey, and grew daily worse & worse in his absence, so that on his return at the end of the month's absence, he saw it was *quite necessary* that immediate steps shd be taken for her removal from home, &, by advice, to the Sea. The babe had been weaned in his absence, but how to leave the children (for she was too ill to go without me and Henry) was matter of great distress. The malady increased rapidly, no sleep, no appetite, and all things wrong in the interior: therefore, on the third of October, (this month) Henry hired a travelling carriage for a fortnight and we arrived at the Stiene Hotel, Brighton, about 6 in the evening after one of the most weary journeys I ever experienced— on the part of the poor, gasping invalid! Her husband, to leave her full room for air in the inside, sat behind the whole way, so that I had far the worst of it, for she said, oh, I shall go into convulsions if I cannot get out! the rain pouring the whole way, yet, at any change of horses she darted out and walked rapidly up and down the road like one distracted. On our arrival we sent for Mr Laurence who ordered a warm bath a blister on the nape of the neck, and other things, and I shall never forget that night, having prevailed on H. to let me be with her as I had slept with her during his absence and was used to watching. Although delightfully housed nr the Sea, at this Hotel we found we could not stand the expence, so, on the third day we came hither and I believe we shall stay, in the whole, 3 weeks.

Since her residence here, we think there is a slight

improvement, and she has great faith in Mr Laurence, but no sleep, or only a few short dosings can be obtained except once perhaps in 5 or 6 nights when her sleep extended to some hours—but we know not how much of this may be attributed to the composing Pills and the numerous draughts she is taking. The [nervous] terrors have, somewhat, abated, but the gloom remains; her inclination to eat has partially returned, but she is afraid to indulge it, for anything solid is felt inconvenient, yet, I am not without hope that she is a little on the mend, and that I shall be able to return home with her on Saturday week 27 October. As Henry has left us for Bath, Frome &c &c it would be almost impossible for him to come hither to escort us back, and if she continues to improve I shall have no difficulty in bringing her up to town but I am in some doubt about her power of bearing the whole 50 Miles in one day. Henry staid ten days with us: 2 of the days he went up to Hampstead to see the children, who, are well taken care of by their good nurse, (a widow of 43) & two other trusty servants, and we have some kind neighbours who call on them and write to us about them.

From the foregoing detail, my dear friend, you will see how impossible it was for H. N. C. to accept y^r kindness: he longs to know you, and does not despair of having that pleasure at some future day. He bears his sore trial nobly, and is tender and generous as Man can be—but his poor wife, now she is able to think a little less of her own innumerable miseries, is fretting about the expence; she cannot bear to take so much of his hard-earned money from him! All the friends at Ottery and elsewhere, write most consolingly, and say, he could do no less, and that she must be easy under it, and think of nothing but getting well. God grant that she may be soon herself again. Before she left H. she wd. sit in a Carriage (wh: we hired by the hour to drive on the Heath with the children and nurses) and never speak one word to the poor babes the whole time.

But now let me present a rather brighter picture. Perhaps Mr Stutfield may have told you that a young Gentleman of the name of Stiemetz at his death, which happened some months since, left my poor S. T. C. a Legacy of £300. I believe he had felt much for his friend at the loss of his Pension, of the Royal Institution: the Gillmans say he was a most amiable youth, and enthusiastically attached to C. I believe Mr Stutfield had introduced him at Highgate. C. sent to the father of the youth to know if his son was of *sound mind* when he made the Will; his answer was, "perfectly." The family is opulent, and young S. wished he could have left more of his property to his beloved friend. I thought it w^d give you pleasure to hear this, and that I still hear good accounts of Hartley, having seen the Leeds Mercury, wherein is advertized the first number of *"The Worthies of Yorkshire & Lancashire"* with Extracts from three of the lives, and the work is highly spoken of: the advertizement says—By Hartley Coleridge—published by Skinner and Bentley, London.

Sara's poor father w^d fain have come with us to Brighton but he was not in travelling trim at the time of our departure nor did Mrs G. *much like* the scheme without the consent of her Husband who is now at Paris for his Health, after a surgical operation, a tumour being cut from the neck; besides, he cannot do [with]out an attendant: Mrs G. used to go with an invalid son, and Col. [?] & others of the family, to Ramsgate: but then he was not as decrepit as he is now and could bathe in the Sea. He receives all your kind messages with a peculiar look of satisfaction, and begins to talk of Stowey and "auld lang syne". We continue to get excellent accounts from Helleston which is cheering to my oppressed mind—and I assure you I felt no small pleasure at the good account you gave of yourself, for I had heard you were far from well. The good folks at K. are amusing the great & gay this Autumn: the letter of last night was franked by the Marquis of Hastings, who with his lively young wife, the late Baroness Grey de Rathyn, only 21--and a nice little Earl of Rawdon, only 9 weeks old, is making some stay in K. The Lady was well known to our folk, for 2 summers ago, she was a long time at K. and was never better pleased than when she was at Greta-hall or on their picnic parties. She then told them, (the girls) that she w^d go again before long for she liked the residence there very much. Edith says, she is doing the same thing which has undone poor Sara, suckling her babe every two hours, and, of course, over-stimulating her digestive powers to keep up the thing. Edith told her of Sara's plight but, "Oh, she is stronger than that Lady, and shall never feel the worse." Her mother is uneasy about her.—Poor Mrs Sandford! the mother of 5 . . [?] . . already! I have rec^d her book and discover a very elegant mind in the

Authoress: she is a wonder! I wish Ly A's Babe had been a son! She will be sorry for poor Sara.

There are several gay folks in Brighton whom we know, S. is in a fright lest they find her out. One lady who lives in the Regency Square has done so; but we cannot profit by her kindness & hospitality. Sara cannot talk.

Owing to my not having yr. last favour before me, I had almost forgotten to thank you for yr. goodness in transcribing the Poems: S. T. C. had no previous copy— the republishing the Poems is his own concern only he is so dilatory he will never do it without help. You did not mention our good friends at Bristol. I trust they are well.

41

Summit House, Stamford Hill: July 24*th* 1833

Dear, and kind friend

Your last, most kind and truly welcome letter was a great comfort to me: I grieve that I cannot send you a cheerful one in return, in the hope of which, I have delayed my thanks much longer than I shd otherwise have done, for I know you do not like to read of the distress of yr friends when it is not in your power to afford relief. Mr Stutfield has perhaps told you of our arrival at this most hospitable and pleasant place; but he could not tell you of the sad result to my poor invalid, of this short journey from Hampstead. The drive was too much for her, as she had not been accustomed to sit up more than a quarter of an hour at one time for the preceding

5 or 6 weeks: she is much lower in spirits & in body much weaker in consequence, and we are in a good deal of anxiety respecting the journey homewards, which, if possible we must try next week, but we must give up altogether a long, and much-desired scheme of Henry's, that of our all going to Eton for six weeks, & occupying the House of his brother Edward there during his absence with his family in his vacation commencing on the 1st of August. Poor Henry thought the change w^d be of use to his poor languid wife; and he delighted in the prospect of Herbert's great enjoyment in the gardens and playing fields where he had passed so many years of his own childhood: but the thing cannot be attempted in Sara's present state; another year she may, (if it be the will of the Almighty!) be in a fitter state to profit from Ed's offer of his house. We spent the month of May at 33 Bedford Square; children & servants and all, except the cook whom we left at Hampstead; here she was under Sir H. Halford, who was sanguine as to her ultimate restoration, and she was better *at first* from his prescriptions, which he varied often before anything w^d agree with her; but I feel persuaded that nothing but time will bring her round again to health, and heaven only knows how long she has yet to suffer! But let me turn to a pleasant subject.

I hope, dear Mr Poole, that you have had all the happiness you anticipated in the society of your beloved niece & her family—perhaps she is still with you:—she is, indeed, a miracle in many ways—but how she can find time with five children to write, and be, as I am informed she is, an active clergyman's wife, is most wonderful to me!

175

I hope she will not endanger her health by too much exertion of mind & body: she was in a delicate state of health when she was living under the same roof at Clifton with our excellent friend Miss Trevenan some years ago: she will be sorry to hear that Miss T. is not at present as strong as she was when she took her journey to the North to be present at Sara's marriage; but she is better than she has been during the last Spring. We were much pleased to hear so good an account of dear Mrs King, and her family: I think I heard that Miss King accompanied Mrs S. to Stowey.

Mr Stutfield, perhaps, told you of the surprizing effort made by y^r old friend, S. T. C. in his recent visit to Cambridge:—Derwent, who came up from Cornwall to be present on that occasion, i.e. the Literary meeting, and who had seen his father a few days previous, at Highgate, was surprized & highly gratified at the unexpected arrival of his father & Mr Gillman with their friend Mr Green on the second day of the meeting: Mr Green took them in his carriage; they were two days on the road, but S. T. C. was so much better that they returned in one! Samuel was most highly gratified with his reception, and pleased to see his College & old haunts once more; he was confined intirely to his bedroom for four months in the beginning of the year.

Mr Powles, our kind host, wishes much to have him over here: but as Sara never takes any one meal with the family but has one drawing room to herself, where I, or one of the Ladies of the family sit with her, I think he wd. not enjoy the visit, so, of course, I have begged him not to

176

send the invitation; but Henry, who is fond of his uncle's society, and proud of introducing him to his friends, wishes him to come. Henry is gone, this day, to Hampstead to see his children & will return through Highgate with news of his Uncle who is just returned from Ramsgate.

If Mr Stutfield had given me a few days notice I shd. have troubled him with a copy of y^r Godson's first volume of Poems, for you: as the book is only value 6^s/ it is not worth while to send it by coach: if you sh^d see it, you will percieve that Hartley has profitted by *yr hint* conveyed to him through a letter from me, in leaving out the last stanza of the Poem "[An Address to Certain] Golden Fishes." I am glad to be able to add, and I know it will please you to see, in the Quarterly Review that the work has been favourably noticed. Mr Murray, whose wife and daughters have a cottage at Hampstead for their health, called [on] us, and good naturedly told us that he had sent off a "Quarterly" to [Leeds] to Hartley, to surprise him, as soon as it was out: I am sure, *I* never was more surprized in my life than when he told us of this piece of kindness:— he was the publisher of Sara's translations—he appeared very sorry for her deplorable illness and said, his daughter w^d be much disappointed at not being able to make her acquaintance. S. T. C. is pleased, and much affected *at the dedication* to himself in his poor son's book: he has not seen him for ten years!—

The reverend John Wood Warter, our nephew elect, has just arrived from Denmark—I have just learnt that he has been at Hampstead where he saw only the children, and I fear he has gone off to the North without our getting a sight of him: I do not know when the marriage is to take place, but shall most likely hear in Bertha's next letter. As Sara goes nowhere, and sees few people, she has not met Mrs Anstice, but we often hear of Mr A. from persons by whom he is admired and esteemed: the Powles's know him. Mrs Stutfield has been so good as to call here to see us, she w^d have liked a sight of poor Sara —but— —

Hampstead, August 2^d. My dear friend, I brought my letter to finish at home thinking you wd like to hear how S. bore the drive—we brought her home in an horizontal position which fatigued her less than on going: she is still in a very weak and low condition; utterly helpless; always on the Sofa, & reading from morning to night. Of course, so much reading is bad for the eyes if they sh^d get as bad as they, once, were she must give up this last *resource* an[d] if she should get any weaker than she now is, she will not be able to hold up the books: we shall be broken-down, *indeed*, if this shd. happen. Henry is always gratified by yr. kind wish to see him at Stowey—I think you w^d like each other: he will see you one of these days! While his parents & other Devon friends live they exact all and every day of his brief holidays—I say "brief", because he is again engaged as last year in the *Register business*.

S. T. C. is ten year younger in spirit: the tepid-salt-water-shower-bath has done wonders! He has passed much of his time at K. with the Lockharts. Mrs L. has a good deal of her father, the late Sir W. Scot, in her, I do not mean, genius, but manners: she has just lost her only sister.

Miss Wordsworth is getting well, to the surprize & joy of all—I fear, we must not expect the return of much strength at 62 years!

S. T. C. will be delighted when I read to him that part of yr. letter, in which he is so affectionately mentioned: what a pity that such friends cannot see more of each other. Sara's love and thanks to you for your pity—Your praise & constant good will! She wants to know if Mrs. S. is strong and if she really can with impunity so constantly employ her head & hands? Your truly obliged affectionate friend

S. COLERIDGE

I beg very kind regards to all my Stowey friends at the head of whom stands Mr Ward—I rejoice in any good tidings you can retale of him. His niece, Mrs W. is gone for 4 months to the land of the Lakes. I hope Mrs Ackland's 2 daughters are both well, and I beg my compliments.

Derwent desired me to thank you for your wish to see him in a former letter of yrs—he has left a great pile of Sermons *for his father to criticise*:—query?

42 *

My dear friend,

The offer of a free conveyance through the kindness of Mr Ward induces me to trouble you with a

* This page has a thick black border. Coleridge died 25th July, 1834.

few lines just to tell you that the day before yesterday Sara had the pleasure of a call from Mrs Sandford who was going to dine in this neighbourhood. Your niece appears to enjoy a perfect state of health and spirits, and although apparently very near confinement, did not appear to suffer the slightest inconvenience. Sara was much pleased at having seen her, but there is little chance, at present, of them seeing much of each other, for Sara, although much better in spirits, is still confined to the sofa from the continued weakness in the back, which is, I am happy to say rather less so within the last 3 months. We were most glad to hear a good report of you, and yours, except of Mr King: I conclude his time of life will not allow his family to cherish much hope of a compleat recovery: this, also, is the case in regard to Henry's parents at Ottery, which place he has only left a week since, having been called there by the alarming alteration in his father's symptoms: he left him rather better, but his weakness rapidly encreases, as well as that of his Lady who is scarcely less in danger than himself, only in a different way.

— I must, now, come to the sad subject that occupies our minds most deeply, at present, the affliction of my good brother & his family at Keswick! (You may possibly have heard something of it.) You know my poor sister has for some years past been in a very uncomfortable state of spirits; her melancholy became much more distressing on Edith's marriage, so that Mrs Lovell wrote me, that she could not bear the mention of her name, but left the room in an agitated manner when it occurred: she

grew more & more irritable & melancholy as the time
drew near of her son's departure for his brother-in-law's
residence in Sussex, whither he was to [be] accompanied
by his father & sister Katharine—in short, about 6 weeks
since, poor S. thought it expedient to carry her to *the*
Retreat at York! I have scarcely heard any particulars of
the state she was in, but I hear from Miss Hutchinson that
force, (Alas,) was become necessary to make her *eat—*
and to *prevent* violence; & he was accompanied on his
woeful journey by a Gentleman, & their old, & faithful
servant, Elizabeth Thomson—who remains with her. As
you may conclude this appalling event has prevented the
intended arrangements of their journey,—they now wait
in hopes that my poor sister may be in a state to be removed in a short time, when S. means to take her & his
whole family to Worthing for an indefinite time, to be as
near Edith as possible; but [as] Edith expects to be confined at the end of this month; & the accounts from York
say, the invalid is *a shade* better, I fear it is not likely they
will be at *Tarring & Worthing* before that time, which, as
far as Kate is concerned, would be desirable but I think
my sister would not be benefitted to be there till after
the expected event.

My dear friend, I know you will sympathize with us in
this sorrow; but you will rejoice to hear that dear S. bears
his trial like a true Christian Philosopher! Miss H. tells us
that Mrs Lovell is wonderfully supported, and Kate, is
her father's own Child; but, at first, Bertha was much
overpowered, and could not be consoled, her terror at her
mother's misery had been so great: but thank heaven! she

has been enabled to rise a little from her dejection & has written to us, which was a great relief to Sara, who is so much attached to them all, that she looks with the greatest anxiety for the accounts which we daily expect, and if letters do not come immediately to us, we get those that are very frequently sent to the Rickman's: *they*, the R's had only left Keswick a few days when the event took place: they had no suspicion that there was anything of derangement in her case. Elizabeth, who writes thrice a week, (or the Physician) says, her Mistress sleeps better, but awakes in a deplorable state: she will now eat voluntary, and thinks it is wicked to refuse food as she, *at first*, did: she knows, perfectly well, where she is, & is surprized at the accommodations around her; & what surprizes me she never asks to return, although they had great difficulty in taking her from the Carriage on arrival. The favorable things in her case, are, that her malady is *not hereditary*; that she is not absorbed by one idea—and her good constitution—*against* her, is her naturally uncheerful disposition, and her age: she is turned of sixty.

Last week I paid a short visit to the Gillmans; they are both in indifferent health & bad spirits: they find it difficult to reconcile themselves to their loss: nineteen years, they say, in the daily habit of seeing & conversing with such a being as he whom they deplore cannot be easily forgotten. They have erected a Tablet in Highgate Church expressive of their love & reverence for the departed.

Farewell my dear & kind friend! I find I must hastily close this incoherent epistle—for Mrs Woolam is ready to set off for London to join her Uncle—to whom my daughter joins me in very kind regards: she begs her *very best* of remembrances to your valued self with mine—& Henry, were he present would heartily unite with these— for he is much gratified that he has been allowed to make your acquaintance. Derwent & his wife and child are well—D. is delighted at having 2 London Boys in his school—a brother of the Judge's is about to send a Boy of 14—in consequence of the report of M^r & Miss Powles —who have visited Helleston this last summer, & have a big Boy in the School. Hartley is much as usual. I have just heard, from Miss Hoare, that Dora Wordsworth is confined to the Sofa with a Spine affection—this is bad news, and, will doubtless withdraw Aunt Hutchinson from the dear folks at Keswick to whom her presence is of great use and consolation. Miss W. is still an invalid, but not unhappy as she has the happiness to have strong nerves. God bless you, my dear Sir—ever your attached

S. COLERIDGE

Henry is about to bring out Conversation—Table Talk of S. T. C. We were quite surprized to find an Extract of the Will in the Papers, and Magazines. H. N. C. thinks Mrs Sandford a delightful person: she converses well.

PRINCIPAL REFERENCES

Coleridge, Berkeley, death of, 1, 26, 32, 84.

Coleridge, Derwent, progress of, 45; a tutor at seventeen, 51; eager to see his father, 56, 84; at Cambridge, 85; improving, 90; unwise activities of, 94; absurd optimism of, 98; a schoolmaster, 109; laziness of, 133; does not show his verses, 121; lectures on Wordsworth, 121; industry of, 138; sermons of, 178; doing well, 183.

Coleridge, Hartley, 1, 8, 13, 16; aged sixteen, 18; aged seventeen, 22-3; going to Oxford, 30; unbalanced habits of, 34; at Oxford, 36; travels outside coach, 45; vacation of, 54; question of his manners, 67; does not show his verses, 68; "elected Fellow" of Oriel, 69; second-class honours of, defended, 71; hopefulness of, 81; disgrace of, 85 f., 138, 141; essays of, 93; unrealised plans of, 94; has no sense of time, 103; "doleful ditty" of, 104; wasted talents of, 111, 133; does not visit Wordsworths, 120; made apprehensive of Poole, 131; "always promising," 138; "consciousness of insufficiency", 140; renounces his past, 143; in debt, 150; leaving the Vale of Grasmere, 166; impossible post for, 167; dedicates Poems to his father, 177; "as usual," 183.

Coleridge, Henry Nelson, lively book by, 97; marriage to Sara Coleridge, 143, 147, 153; bad health of, 161; editing S. T. C.'s Poems, 168; editing *Table Talk*, 183.

Coleridge, Samuel Taylor, his absence in Germany, 1 ff.; gay life there, 4; obscure politics of, 5; delays of, 6-9; quarrel with Stoddart (of Malta), 9; verses of, in bad taste, 10; death of *The Friend*, 11, 14; educating his children, 12; ought to rouse himself, 14, 28; quarrel with Wordsworth, 16; "airy castles" of, 17; lectures of, 20; "desertion" of, 32; plans of, 33; and opium, 33, 48, 165; *Biographia*, 36; news of, 40; *Zapolya*, 43; its failure, 47; disappoints, also, with "*Koula-Khan*," 48; in 1817, 66; in his "better way", 73; improving, 107; *Aids to Reflection*, preparing, 114, 128, 125; nominated to Literary Society, 116; in 1825, 120, 122; new verses of, 136; and Sir G. Beaumont's will, 137; death of brother George, 142; 1828 *Poems*, 142; *Aids to Reflection* admired, 135; decline of, 146; *Church and State*, 148, 155; becomes grandfather, 165; legacy for, 172; surprizing visit to Cam:, 176; good result of salt-water bath on, 178; Gillmans confused by death of, 182.

Coleridge, Mrs, on *Lyrical Ballads*, 4, 5; on "this painting business", 19; on an illness at Keswick, 25; on life at Keswick, 27, 29, 38, 60, 62 ff., 75; on withdrawal of Wedgwood annuity,

Principal References

THE END

1934
PRINTED IN GREAT BRITAIN
BY R. & R. CLARK LTD. EDINBURGH